PETER
ABELARD

Books by Helen Waddell

BEASTS AND SAINTS

THE DESERT FATHERS

MEDIAEVAL LATIN LYRICS

PETER ABELARD

THE WANDERING SCHOLARS

PETER ABELARD

A NOVEL BY HELEN WADDELL

DRAWINGS BY LASZLO MATULAY

NEW YORK: HENRY HOLT AND COMPANY

CONTENTS

BOOK I

THE CLOISTER OF NOTRE DAME

June 1116–May 1117

CHAPTER I

"Temps s'en va,
Et rien n'ai fait" . . .

ABELARD raised his head. It was a pleasant voice, though a little drunken, and the words came clearly enough, a trifle blurred about the consonants, to the high window of the Maison du Poirier. The window was open, for the June night was hot, and there were few noises after ten o'clock in the Place du Parvis Notre Dame.

"Time goes by,
And naught do I.
Time comes again,
. . . Et ne fais rien!"

Abelard's smile broadened. "I am very sure, my friend," said he, "that you do not." But at any rate he had found a good tune. The listener's ear was quick. He began noting it on the margin of his manuscript, while his brain busied itself fitting Latin words to the original: a pity to waste so good a tune and so profound a sentiment on a language that was the breath of a day.

"Fugit hora,
Absque mora,
Nihil facio" . . .

Not to that tune. The insinuating, if doomed, vernacular lilted again. Abelard realized that he was spoiling the

[3]

margin of his Commentary on Ezekiel, and turned back resolutely.

"*Now, as Augustine says, our concern with any man is not with what eloquence he teaches, but with what evidence.*" But the thread of his argument was broken: he got up and came over to the window. The singing had stopped, but he could see the tonsured head below him, glimmering like a mushroom in the dusk, while the legs tacked uncertainly across the broad pavement of the Parvis Notre Dame on their way to the cheerful squalors of the Petit Pont. Suddenly they halted: the moon had come out from a drifting haze, and the singer, pausing on the edge of a pool of light, peered at it anxiously, and then lifted up his eyes. The voice rose again, chastened, this time in the venerable cadences of the hymn for dawn:

"Jam lucis orto sidere
Statim oportet bibere."

"The blasphemous pup," said Abelard. He leaned out, to hear the rest of it:

"Now risen is the star of day.
Let us arise and drink straightway.
That we in peace this day may spend,
Drink we and drink, nor make an end."

This was a better parody, because a simpler, than the one he had made upon it himself ten years ago, to illustrate for his students the difference between the accidents and the essential, the accidents being the words, the essential the tune. Lord, the Blessed Gosvin's face when he began singing it! Doubtless he would be the Blessed Gosvin some day: so holy a youth could not fail of a

[4]

sanctified old age. St. Gosvin perhaps: the youngster was Prior already at . . . he had forgotten where. The impudent, smooth-faced prig.

Abelard's mind was running down a channel it knew and did not like: the moment in the classroom at St. Geneviève, when Gosvin's reedy treble had interrupted the resonant voice from the rostrum with those innocent questionings, answered contemptuously, the master's eyes half averted and his mind less than half attentive, till the sudden horrid silence brought him to his senses and he realized that he was trapped, even as he had so often trapped that good old goat, William of Champeaux. He had recovered, magnificently; but for the moment he had felt the hounds at his throat. And the cheering had been too vehement: they knew. Somebody on the Ile de Cité that night made a song about David and Goliath, not a very good song, but the name had stuck to him since, though not many remembered the origin of it. A pity, all the same, that Gosvin took to the cloister. It would be very pleasant to have him lecturing to empty benches at St. Geneviève, while at Notre Dame the students wedged open the doors and stood thick on the stairs. Thanks to that one trick, the pup will go all his life thinking he has a better brain than Master Peter Abelard, and he will tell the story to his novices, how the Lord once aided him, and he but a lad, to defend the truth, and one of them will write his life after he is dead, and pretend that there would have been a greater philosopher than Peter Abelard, if God had not called the Blessed Gosvin to holiness.

Oh, enough. The folly of it, to be in one's thirty-seventh year and writhe like a worm in salt at a trifle that happened ten years ago. One forgot; and in a flash the agony came again, as if it were yesterday. Heaven knew there had been triumphs enough, before and since, to take that taste from his mouth. Poor William! William had driven him from Paris, and in the end he had driven William to the cloister, and now William was a bishop. Well, he had Abelard to thank for that, and his sermons might easily be better than his lectures. And old Anselm at Laon: sheep every one of them, with their meek faces, browsing over and over the old close-bitten pastures, with their "St. Augustine saith . . . St. Jerome saith . . . The Blessed Gregory saith . . ." As if one could not prove anything, and deny it, and prove it back again, out of St. Augustine alone. Some time he would do it, for a testimony unto them. Pit the Fathers one against the other. Smash the whole blind system of authority and substitute . . . Master Peter Abelard? said the mocking voice within him. He shook his head, suddenly humble. Not that. Not that. But a reasonable soul. *The spirit of man is the candle of the Lord.* Abelard shuddered and was still. It was about him again, the dark immensity, the pressure of some greatness from without upon his brain, and that within which struggled to break through to it. *I said, Ye are gods.*

Behind him the room darkened. The flame of the candle sank, leaped and went out, and the abominable smell of a burnt-out wick reeked into the air. Abelard woke, cursed, and thrust the inkpot upon it. That dog, Guibert, where had he put the candles? The shiftless fool. But no bigger fool than himself, to keep the swine about the place.

"Guibert! Guibert!"

There was no answer. Abelard stumbled over a footstool, opened the door, and shouted down the stairs to the cupboard where Guibert slept when he was not employing his leisure in the Quartier. The door gaped open: the frowsy bed lay huddled as Guibert had that morning risen from it. Caterwauling again, said Abelard: though what the women see in him . . . Flatters them, I suppose, the way he does me, he thought ruefully. But there was something about him . . . that dog's gaze of his, the tail at half-mast to go erect or clapped to its hindquarters, according to the look in your eye. And after all it was twenty years: twenty years since the pair of them had clattered down the stony track from Le Palais to go to Paris. What was it that Irishman wrote the other day? *In those first days when youth in me was happy and life was swift in doing, and I wandering through the divers cities of sweet France for the love I had of learning, gave all my might to letters.* They were good days. But no better, nor so good, as these. Abelard had come back to the window: it was too dark to read, and too early to sleep. He stood watching the jagged line of the roofs of St. Geneviève against the sky. They had driven him from Paris, and he had gone to St. Geneviève, and emptied the schools of Notre Dame. He had gone to Melun, and Paris had come to Melun. He had gone to Laon for theology—Gilles de Vannes had lifted his eyebrows at him and said, "Philosophy is my washpot: over Theology also will I cast out my shoe!"—and Paris had implored him to itself again. And now? He stood chewing the cud of old triumphs, anticipating fresh ones, omnipotence mounting higher in his heart. No need now to be a peripatetic philosopher: the world came to Paris, to him.

[7]

PETER ABELARD

Two Masters of Arts from Padua, a Doctor of Laws from Bologna, a handful of young men from Salamanca, a couple of Malachy's men from Armagh, a rabble of English and Germans, and half the youngsters of France, from Bec to Montpellier and Toulouse. Yet some day he must see Rome. Plato said it would be well for that state whose king was a philosopher. What of Christendom, if a philosopher were Pope?

The wave of power swept up: he swung on the crest of it, indifferent as a strong swimmer. And swaying there, his mind began challenging the enigma of that other scholar, that Gerbert who also became Pope, though for three years only, till he died. Necromancer, devil-aided, devil-destroyed, said the legend, and all, Thierry of Chartres used to say, because he had a head for mathematics, and had studied Arabic and geometry at the schools of the Saracens. It was hard to come at any truth about him: but there, Abelard had always felt, was a man with whom he would have been on terms. The stories of his learning and his devilry might be equally fabulous, but he had written his own memorial in one line of his epitaph for Boethius:

> "That intellect divine
> Compels for thee the world's imperium."

Not intellect only, perhaps. Chicane and intrigue, as well as sheer momentum of genius. There was that ugly story of the archbishopric of Rheims. Abelard moved impatiently, his mind twitching away from the thought of it, the whispering, the smooth-faced strategy, the whole corroding business of administration, the pygmy warfare of dean and chapter. He had seen enough of it already, since they made him Canon of Notre Dame. There was ordination too. Was it of Gerbert they told the story, how the pains of Hell took hold on him, saying his last Mass in the Jerusalem chapel at Rome, and the chalice slipped from his hands, and the wine fell like great gouts of blood, dripping from step to step of the altar stairs? He drew his mind away. Not yet. He could not yet set his hands about the Host.

The wave of omnipotence was receding. Abelard dropped on the chest by the window, his head resting on the sill. He knew only that he was very tired. Denise in Brittany used to hold his head between her hands when he was like this. Odd that when one was tired it was the only thing that brought some ease. Was that why the dying go more easily if someone will hold their hands? He shook himself, and stood up, to go to bed. The moon was higher now, and the shadow of Notre Dame had moved, revealing something that had shown only as a blot of darkness against the wall of the Cloister. It stirred: the shadow became two shadows: for a moment the moon shone on a girl's upturned face, blanched in its light. Then the other shadow stooped over it, and they were one shadow again. Abelard stood looking down, his mouth contemptuous. Yet there was a quality in the rigidity of those silent figures that held him. He could not reach them. Time was with him. Eternity flowed about those two.

Twelve. At the first stroke the two shivered apart. The girl ran like a lapwing across the steps of Notre Dame, and towards the Rue Sainte Marine. The man came steadily enough across the Parvis, and under the projecting houses. A moment later, and Abelard heard his stealthy foot upon the stair. So it was Guibert who had inhabited eternity a moment since. With a hearty re-action of disgust, Abelard flung open the door, and an avalanche of malediction volleyed down the stair.

CHAPTER II

GILLES DE VANNES, Canon of Notre Dame, sat sunk in his great chair asleep. His massive chin lay in creases on his chest: every line of him sagged downwards. On the table at his elbow stood a pasty, a surprisingly small segment of it cut: beside it, an empty flagon. Abelard, looking down upon him, wondered for the hundredth time how he could so love anything so gross. Yet there was an innocence about the Canon as he slept: the watcher's heart softened. Almost he could for-bear to waken him. But he was restless: he had come for conversation and he meant to have it. He turned to kick the log upon the fire, for the unwieldy bulk in the great chair took little exercise, and was chilly, even in June.

"Not a pleasant sight," agreed a rich voice behind him.

Abelard started, and turned. The small, shrewd eyes twinkled up at him, pin-points of intelligence in the vast encompassing of the flesh.

"Yet awake," the husky voice went on, "the eyes do but increase the resemblance to the pig."

Abelard took it manfully. "I did not come here," he said, "to hear my own thoughts repeated to me. I came for yours."

"You are an honester young man than when I first knew you," said the Canon. "But you will never be as

honest as myself. What did you come for? Your dinner?"
He indicated the pasty.

Abelard sat down, and pulled it towards him. "I was
not hungry," he began.

"But you are now," said the Canon. "Guibert had made
you an omelette, and the grease stood on it in flakes, and
it tasted of hen's turds rather than of hen's eggs."

"It is true," said Abelard. "I do not know why all his
food tastes so. I have seen him wash the platters, and
even the pots. For a long time I thought it was that."

"But he does not wash the cloth that washes the pots,"
said Gilles. "There is no flavor quite like it."

"There is no flavor like the flavor of this pasty," said
Abelard. He was eating ravenously.

"It is a pleasure to feed you, Peter," said Gilles. "Not
only because you have the air of a hungry hawk, but
because you have discrimination. A sensualist, like myself."

"God forbid," said Abelard, his mouth full.

"It is true," said the Canon. "That you live on herrings'
tails with that scarecrow of yours across the way is but
an accident." He had risen with difficulty, lumbered over
to the dresser, and was carefully filling a goblet for his
guest. "Some day you will put your mind to good living.
You have the palate, and the disposition for it. Everything but application. And opportunity."

"I do not know," said Abelard, reaching for the cup,
"why I visit you."

"To do you justice"—Gilles let himself down in his
chair—"it is not only for the food. But you find in my
conversation the same quality that you find in that pasty.
It is high, but there is pimento in it. Also you see in me

the satisfaction of your own desires. Vicariously, you savor in me the richness of living that your wits deny you."

"You have wits enough, yourself," said Abelard.

"Not for philosophy, young man. I took to the classics. For I am a sensualist in my mind as well as in my body. That is where we differ. Your mind snuffs up the east wind. That is why you are as lean as the kine of Pharaoh. But there is hope for you. I was once as lean as you, and fasted, I dare be sworn, a deal more often, till I was past grace."

"I have wondered sometimes," said Abelard, "if you ever knew it."

"Grace?" said the Canon. "Aye. But—is it Jerome, or Ambrose? 'The sirens have the faces of women, because nothing so estrangeth the heart from the love of God as the faces of women.' Not Jerome. Too crude. The Blessed Gregory, perhaps. And after that, there was this." He indicated the empty flagon with finger-tips of surprising delicacy. "Messer Gaster, we despise him in youth, but though the amorists will not have it, he is the master-organ of our pleasures. He is the first thought of our infancy, and I verily believe he will be the last of our age."

Abelard moved impatiently. "I do not believe it," he said. "Anyhow, not of you. It is the movement of your wits you live by, that itching tongue, that rubs itself against the bark."

Gilles reflected. "It seems to me," he said meditatively, "that I fill my mind even as I fill my belly: *bonnes bouches:* jelly of quinces and salted almonds. . . .

> "Mere breath of flutes at eve,
> Mere seaweed on the shore."

The husky voice was suddenly resonant. Abelard sat motionless. This was the incantation for which he came.

> "A jar of the Albana, nine years old,
> Still a full amphora. And in the garden
> There's parsley, Phyllis, for twining coronals,
> And trails of ivy
> To bind your shining hair."

There was a long silence. The Canon's small eyes turned from the fire and rested, very kindly, on the man opposite him. The impatient hands were still, the nervous frown had gone from between the brows, but wistfulness still hovered. Thirty-seven? A schoolboy, thought Gilles, a schoolboy of thirteen. But to be humored.

"Your last lecture today?"

"It was." Abelard roused, awake.

"I heard it," said Gilles, "or rather, the effect of it. The like of the hubbub was a scandal. Is it true that they took you in your chair upon their shoulders?"

"They may have thought," said Abelard gravely, "of putting me in the Seine. But they set me on my own doorstep instead."

"And then you made them a speech?"

Abelard flushed. "I did."

"I heard it," said the Canon, chuckling gently. "Very pretty, my dear, very pretty. The human reason the habitation of God with men? John Scotus Erigena said something very like it, three hundred years ago: but with less grace. They killed him for it in the end, you know. Stabbed him to death with their pens. Like Hypatia. And that reminds me, what think you of our own?"

"Our own?"

"Hypatia. Heloise. And the lovelier name of the two, after all."

"Heloise? Fulbert's niece? He was hours telling me how she was coming home from the convent. Tedious old man. Well, what of her? Priscian in petticoats?"

Gilles was looking into the fire. When he spoke, it was as if to himself:

> "Mere breath of flutes at eve,
> Mere seaweed on the shore."

"And what," said Abelard, unreasonably irritated, "precisely do you mean by that?"

"The same texture," said Gilles, still brooding. "It is not color, it is not even line; it is the surface that is perfection. Though there is line: too straight at the moment, but she's young. Seventeen, they say. Not much color, and she does not yet amend it. I like a white-faced wench myself. The eyes show better, so. Why do fools say, black as night? There's more color in a night sky than ever there is at noonday. Stars, too."

Abelard rose to his feet. He was frowning.

"You seem acquainted with this Phoenix," he said drily.

"Her uncle has brought her here," said Gilles placidly. "She borrows my books. She has my Persius now. A strange taste in a woman. Difficult too. But not for her."

"She reads with you, then?"

"Aye. And old Fulbert sits there, doting on her, till he sleeps."

"Hence your knowledge of the texture," said Abelard.

The Canon meditated, balancing two orders of thought. The impishness vanished from his eye.

"Young man," he said suddenly, "are there finger-

[14]

marks in my books? Winestains, and the smudge of a greasy thumb?"

"There are not. My own are a deal the dirtier of the two."

"I can imagine it," said the Canon drily.

Abelard came across the room to him. He was crimson.

"Sir," he said, "forgive me. It was unpardonable. I thought—"

"The foulest pig of the Epicurean sty?" said the Canon gently. "In short, that I was I?" He dismissed it with a gesture of the finger-tips. "But look here, Master Peter. You say you find Fulbert tedious. You have said it, I think, of every one of our canons, barring, I believe, myself. And you are justified. But a man makes enemies so. And a philosopher can have as many enemies as the Prince of Darkness. He thrives on them. But bishops do not, nor the great ones."

"I believe," said Abelard slowly, "that you have the Prince of Darkness himself to fetch and carry for you."

The Canon shook his head. "Not the Prince of Darkness. Original sin only. They are not to be confounded. So have a care. Moreover, it might be as well now and then to come to chapter. You miss some good things, else. This morning—" He chuckled ruefully. "Poor Evrard!"

"He that married his housekeeper?"

"Aye. The Bishop had written to Ivo of Chartres for his finding. You know Ivo?"

"I have seen him."

"I was at the schools with him. That was a man. A face like a rock. I never knew the man could tell a bawdy story to Ivo of Chartres. But kind. There was a girl would not marry the man her parents chose, and they brought her to Ivo to force her. 'That is not marriage,' said he, 'which is the coition of two bodies, but the union of two souls.' "

"And which," said Abelard blandly, "does he find the union of Evrard and his housekeeper?"

Gilles's eyelids flickered. "Our Bishop had not concerned himself with that aspect, but with the question of Evrard's emoluments."

"Well?"

"Ivo says that the canon who marries loses his benefice."

"And privilege?"

"Not privilege. They cannot take the tonsure from us for marriage. But the profit of it, yes. Ivo's argument is that the faithful layman does not support us to live precisely as he does."

"I think," said Abelard slowly, "that I am with Ivo."

"You would be," said the Canon. "And so am I." He met his friend's astonishment with a tranquil eye. "What puzzles me," he went on meditatively, "is his marrying her. That he should have found it necessary."

CHAPTER III

YOU may go your ways, Fulbert. You may go your ways. Not one foot will you get me from my chair this day."

"But consider—"

Gilles de Vannes twinkled up at the little agitated figure through half-closed eyelids.

"And do not wag your finger at me. What does the

man look like? A wasp trying to convert a caterpillar."
He subsided into rumbling chuckles.

"A wasp?" Fulbert stiffened, his face pink. He flushed
easily, for he had the exquisite sensitive skin of the aged
ecclesiastic.

"There, there, Fulbert. Not a wasp: a bee. Man, it is
the consecrated metaphor for the good ecclesiastic. *Apis
humilis, casta, indefatigabilis*—but you must not sting,
Fulbert. It does not matter for wasps: it is their function.
But bees die of it. Lord, Lord, do you remember poor
Evrard's first letter, begging to be received? From Liege,
I think. 'Having, as an unworthy pup, licked up sufficient
crumbs from under the table here, I would fain enter
your lordship's hive as an obedient bee.' "

Fulbert received the pleasantry with an inclination. He
had a little relaxed, but formality never left him. "I have
never understood," he said, "the circumstances in which
Evrard became one of us. Whatever our faults. we were,
I think, a body not without distinction."

Gilles's eyes caressed him. It was a joy to see anyone
derive so much innocent pleasure from his office. "His
guilelessness," he said briefly. "It was in Fulco's time, you
remember. And Fulco, may God assoil him, needed an
animal of some kind in the chapter. Evrard was the only
one of us who did what he was told. He has been like a
lost dog since Fulco died. Nobody ever tells him anything. And so— Poor Evrard!"

"I confess," said Fulbert, "that I have some difficulty
in comprehending your position. You gave your vote
with the rest of us in chapter, after the reading of the
letter from Ivo of Chartres?"

"I did."

[17]

"Yet you refuse to attend the chapter which deprives him."

"I think," said Gilles thoughtfully, "that I have always preferred theory to practice."

"You do not then, in your heart, agree with Ivo of Chartres?"

"With all my heart," said Gilles fervently. "God forbid that the Cloître Notre Dame should become a nursery of squalling brats."

"In that case—"

"I tell you, Fulbert," said Gilles, roused to brief energy, "I have no liking for executions of justice. Doubtless it is a bad conscience. For I am never the executioner or the spectator, but the wretch that is tied to the pillar."

"This is no question of the discipline," said Fulbert stiffly. "Evrard is a canon, and not a choir-boy. And a simple act of ecclesiastical deprivation—"

"I never liked," said Gilles, "to see a man ashamed. Odd," he continued, musing, "for I have never in my life been ashamed of myself. Except of course," he added gravely, "on such occasions as the rubric demands it."

Fulbert nodded approvingly. He rose.

"I am to make your excuses, then?"

"You are a good fellow, Fulbert," said Gilles gratefully. "Tell them it is a profound sciatica. It was the truth yesterday. Only yourself will know it is a bad conscience." He sighed. "Not many of us, Fulbert, are like you, with a conscience as candid as your hair."

The sensitive face flushed to the silver ring of the tonsure.

"There," said Gilles tenderly, "I have embarrassed you with my praises."

"I shall be late," said Fulbert piteously. He looked about him in distress. "Where did I— Surely— Heloise!"

The girl reading at the further window laid down her book and came swiftly down the long room. Gilles sat watching her as she came. She wore green, girdled low; her hair fell on either side the oval of her face, and swung in long plaits to her knee.

One of the dead queens, alive and young, the stone queens for the west portal of Chartres: one of them, the loveliest and saddest, wore her hair so. But here there was no sadness yet: the laughter that sprang in her at sight of these two together rippled in her face as light glances in water. Gilles glanced at Fulbert, and mentally absolved him. This radiant creature could never have been begotten by the spinsterish figure nervously fidgeting with its hood. She was beside him now, touching him with her light fingers, turning back his over-long sleeves, settling his collar: and the creature stood there happy and quiescent, blinking, thought Gilles savagely, like ˄ tom-cat on a sunny wall.

"Thank you, my dear, thank you. You always know what I want. You will go straight home, sweetheart?"

"Must she go, Fulbert?" said Gilles abruptly. "Leave her with me while you are in chapter. There is a fair draft of the inscription for the lapidaries to make, and gout in my thumb, and Heloise has the best clerk's script in Paris."

"Surely, surely," Fulbert babbled with pleasure. "You think the girl writes well, Gilles?"

"If Adam does but copy in stone what she writes on vellum, it will be a rare marvel," said Gilles.

"I will come back for her," said Fulbert, "when chapter

is over. And then I can tell you, Gilles, tell you all about
it."

"That was my hope," said Gilles gravely. "But I had
not liked to ask it of so busy a man. It would be a great
kindness. And indeed, Fulbert," he called, as the Canon
fumbled with the latch, "I would come with you to the
stoning of Stephen if I had the courage."

"Not Stephen," corrected Fulbert kindly, "Evrard."

"I grow old. I grow old." Gilles sank back despondent
in his chair. His junior by five years beamed upon him,
making deprecatory noises, and the door latched behind
him. The two pairs of eyes met.

"Heloise," said Gilles de Vannes suddenly, "you are
the only contemporary I have."

Heloise nodded. She drew a stool beside his feet, and
sat looking into the fire.

"I know," she said after a pause. "And yet I feel it
with a difference. It is as though you had all time behind
you as well. So that I can ask you things."

"What things?"

"I am always asking you things. But today—" She hesitated, her eyes on the white wood ash.

Gilles waited, content to look at her.

"Gilles," she spoke suddenly, "what will become of
Evrard?"

"I think," he said slowly, "he will do very well. It so
happens that there is a school of sorts at Sarzeau, and the
priest has little of letters, and I have some influence there.
It will not be much of a living, but better than going to
feed hogs for the woman's people. They are farmers. He
had thought of that, God help him."

"He came to see you, then?"

"I went to see him," said Gilles reluctantly.

Heloise turned her eyes on the motionless bulk in the great chair, a caress of tenderness so profound that now, thought Gilles, it is I who blink like a cat. Then her face hardened.

"Gilles, was he wrong to marry?"

"Canonically, yes."

"Then is marriage a sin?"

"Not a sin. Only a mistake." She was looking at him, and the delighted irony in her eyes met the irony in his. "That," he continued, "is why the canonists regard it so gravely. For one can repent and be absolved of a sin, but there is no canonical repentance for a mistake. Unless indeed in the sense wherein St. Paul said: 'Such shall have trouble in the flesh: but I spare you.'"

The light danced in her face, and suddenly went out. "But Evrard—it was such a good face, and she—I saw her this morning at her door, all sodden with crying and frightened. And the Archdeacon—my uncle says it was he who first denounced him in chapter—the Archdeacon—" She stopped.

"Has strange bedfellows," agreed Gilles smoothly.

Heloise had risen, her hands clenched in sudden fury. "Then *why?* And yet you, you voted against Evrard."

"And should vote again tomorrow." The indulgence had gone from Gilles's voice and left it cold.

It had its effect. The girl sat down again, as if suddenly spent, gazing into the changing heart of the fire as if she followed there the tortuous working of men's minds. Gilles reached out his hand and turned the hour-glass.

"Say it, Heloise. Say what you are thinking me."

[21]

She shook her head. "I do not want to say it, because
I know it is not true."

"What is not true?"

"That you are a hypocrite."

"I am," said Gilles. "Officially, I am a canon of Notre
Dame, and I have the morals, and, what is worse, the
appearance, of Silenus."

Heloise shook her head. "It is not that. You make no
pretense at goodness. Not like the Archdeacon. But—you
condemned Evrard."

"Canon law condemned him. So also would it condemn the Archdeacon, if the charges against him were
first brought, and then proved. And it is easier to prove
marriage than . . . other forms of depravity."

"And the Church says marriage is a sacrament."

"And I believe," said Gilles steadily, "in the Holy
Catholic Church."

Heloise drew a long breath of bewilderment. "Gilles,"
she said suddenly, shaking the canonical riddle from her
shoulders, "tell me. What do you, yourself, think of
marriage?"

Gilles turned from fingering the hour-glass and gazed
steadily into the eyes confronting him. His heavy jaw
set.

"Marriage, to me, is a compromise with the flesh. The
Church in its great wisdom has given its blessing to that
compromise, considering it, moreover, as an indulgence
that brings its own chastening, and speaking also, as did
Ivo of Chartres, of a certain spiritual union, of which I
have seen little, and have, I confess, desired less. But the
very root of marriage, to me, is the satisfying of a lust of
the flesh: and the Church itself declares that the ascetic

has chosen the more excellent way. I am no ascetic, but my satisfactions have never had the blessing of the Church upon them. Which is perhaps illogical," his voice was lightening, "since I have never eaten without a *Benedicat*."

"Then is love lust?"

"Its root is lust."

For a while neither spoke.

"You find that horrible?"

"I do." Her voice was almost inaudible.

"But the rose is lovelier than its root, Heloise. And by your leave, madam, a rose grows better in a dunghill than in a quarry of white Carrara marble. And dies . . ."—he hesitated, and the words came grating—"and dies less soon."

Heloise turned upon him, her mouth quivering.

"Dies?"

Gilles shook his head. "This also will pass. And marriage—marriage seems to me the effort to make that permanent which is in its nature transient. *Nequidquam, nequidquam*, in vain, in vain."

His face had sunk into its heaviest lines of disillusionment.

> 'Hunger and thirst appeased, there's profit in't.
> The body's richer for it: but from this,
> All human beauty and the face of men,
> Naught but the ghosts of unfulfilled desire
> Drifting on every wind.'

The husky voice grating through the heavy Lucretian hexameters had strengthened, till the whole plangent resonance of desire rang in it like a violin. Heloise sat motionless, her eyes unfathomable with pain, fixed on the

[23]

dreamer's face. Another listener unseen in the doorway, the arras clutched in his hand, stood halted, holding his breath.

> "Never yet
> Hath he possessed her wholly, never yet
> Have twain been one."

Nequidquam, nequidquam. The voice stumbled on the sullen consonants and ceased. Gilles sat forward, his head sunk on his breast, his hands hanging from his knees. With a long sigh Heloise stirred and woke, to meet the eyes of Abelard, still rigid in the shadow of the door.

CHAPTER IV

IT was long after sunset, but the crescent moon above Notre Dame was still no more than a glimmering sickle in the harvest glow of the sky. The inner radiance that is the mystery of the light of the Ile de France slept on its towers. Abelard, rounding the last bend above the Clos des Vignerons, halted in the stride that had carried him through twenty miles of the Seine valley. Often as he had seen it, this beauty never failed to catch him by the throat. Before him rode the island with its towers, glimmering like some great white-sailed ship that he had seen, bearing into Nantes from the vast spaces of the open Loire, or a wild swan, resting a moment in mid flood. It had the air of a winged victory, stayed of its own volition in its imperious way. "Queen among cities, moon among stars," his brain was beating out the lovely rhythms, "island of royal palaces: and in that island hath

Philosophy her royal and ancient seat, who alone, with
Study her sole comrade, holding the eternal citadel of
light and immortality, hath set her victorious foot on the
withering flower of the fast-aging world."

The withering flower. The light on the banks had
dimmed, the river darkened, but still the island glowed
with that unearthly light, as though its fountains were
within. Abelard swung down the river road, his blood
pulsing in a strange exaltation that was the climax of his
mood. Never had he so felt the richness of living as in
these last days, never been so joyously aware of the urge
of creation. The name of his new book had flashed on
him, *Sic et Non,* and he had stood astonished and charmed
at its simplicity and its absoluteness. His scholars were
out of Paris, but he had hardly been aware of the emptiness of his days, for he had plunged headlong into a re-
reading of the Fathers, and the surge of St. Augustine's
prose rose and fell in his brain. He was drinking little
and eating less, but something was wine in his blood, and
all the day and half the night reading could not daunt
the restlessness that fevered him. Today it had driven
him out, but the miles of the Seine valley had only set
his pulse beating to a headier rhythm. Paris rode there
to greet him, unearthly and proud: but the man who
swung down the river-path to enter it came as both con-
queror and lover.

The river ran dark below the Petit Pont: Abelard's
countryman's nostrils twitched as he came through the
narrow street between the crowding houses. Thank
Heaven the chapter had insisted that Raoul Testart
should at least close in his latrines: the river that had been
a sheet of silver here ran like a sewer. What sort of

creature was man, that he could not live without a heap of ordure? The air grew sweeter as he passed into the wide Parvis, but the light was dim beneath the tall houses, and as he entered his own doorway, he stumbled in the black well of the stairs. It was at once close and chill. Guibert had fried some abomination for his supper: the smell of burnt fat still hung in the air. His own room was heavy with it; his manuscripts lay in a disordered heap on the table, pushed to one side to make room for the platter with its revolting gobbets of flesh congealed upon it. Guibert had long since disappeared. Abelard's stomach, never a strong one, rose. He took a hasty pull at the flagon, cut himself a hunch of bread and cheese and went over to the window to eat it, the demi-god who had swung through the radiant dusk become an irritable and queasy-stomached scholar.

The loneliness of the room gathered about him: in the dreary reaction after exaltation, Abelard could have groaned aloud. The books looked on him with indifferent faces: his manuscript was a meaningless huddle of words. He would go to Gilles: the thought of the man warmed you like a wine. In a moment he was on the stairs, almost as though something chased him, across the Parvis, through the great arch of the cloister gate, and climbing the familiar stair. His hand on the door, a sudden reluctance seized him, a memory of sensation so violent that for a moment it sickened him: but he thrust it down and, opening the door, drew an involuntary breath of relief. Gilles was alone. The great chair at the hearth was empty, and white ash lay on the stone. Gilles himself stood at the window, craning to catch the last of the light on a page of parchment held close to his eyes. Abelard crossed to him lightly, and stood at his side.

"Humph," said Gilles, without looking up. He finished his paragraph, laid down the parchment, and turned his eyes on Abelard, a gaze of slow kindliness that wrapped his shivering loneliness like a cloak. He forgot his darkness and discouragement: he could have kissed Gilles's hands in gratitude.

"I was a fool to stay away," he blundered out.

"So that was it," said Gilles.

"I did not know I was doing it. Gilles, do you remember what Marbod of Angers said about a man losing the truth of himself?"

"Juvenal first, I think. But that is a trifle. Well?"

"I find it again, the truth of myself, with you."

Gilles considered him.

"The pit of your stomach more likely." He turned from him and went over to the dresser. "By the look of you, you last broke your fast this time yesterday. They stuff this," he was busy carving a great ham, "in Brittany better than anywhere. And the wine, like your quotation, is from Angers. But I should commend you to eat before you drink."

Abelard came over meekly for his platter and carried it to the window-seat. In a moment Gilles followed him, with two tankards, and set himself down on the settle.

"It is perhaps no wonder," he said meditatively, "that Fulbert is concerned for your health."

Abelard looked up, startled. "Fulbert?"

"My good Peter, you have been the god of their idolatry to many young men: but it is a triumph to have captured anything so dry. He talks of nothing else.

[27]

Hercules for strength, because you carried him out of chapter; but there is nothing pagan that is Christian enough for your handling of him afterwards—"

Abelard moved uncomfortably. "I knew nothing of it," he said sulkily, "till he slid down beside me in the stalls. And when I lifted him, it was like handling a little dead bird. He came to, pretty quickly; but I did not like to let him walk home alone."

"And so you carried him?"

"I did not. I only gave him an arm."

"By this time, you carried him like St. Christopher, and put him in his bed, and even thought to come here and fetch Heloise, and went and sat with him every day till he was about again, meantime discoursing like St. Augustine and St. Jerome, with the wisdom of the Blessed Gregory thrown in."

"For heaven's sake, Gilles— But you know yourself there is something about him."

"There is," said Gilles, "and I shall tease you no longer. I told you you were neglecting him."

"It is not his conversation," said Abelard, "for he has none. Is it his innocence?"

"I think myself," said Gilles, "that he has more of the faculty of admiration than any man I have ever known. He has never ceased to wonder at finding himself a canon of Notre Dame; like Ausonius, when they made him consul. A canon's stall is a sacred thing to him; he thinks better of himself ever since. And I have never known a man with so small a tincture of letters and so profound a reverence for them. He was always by way of regarding you as a demigod; and now that you have condescended, he goes scarlet and stammers when he speaks of you."

"You have seen him?"

"He was here yesterday, lonely, for Heloise had gone for a while to Argenteuil. He sent her, for he thought her too much confined in the nursing of him. And he spoke of nothing else, unless indeed it was your scoundrel of a Guibert."

"You see," said Abelard, "it is not easy to know what to talk about. And when he asked me what Guibert paid for his fish—"

"It is a careful soul," said Gilles. "The tears stood in his eyes when he told me what your housekeeping cost you. He could feed you, he says, on a quarter of the sum, and you would be as sleek as Shadrach, Meshach, and Abednego."

Abelard sighed. "I never seem to have any money," he said ruefully, "and I never have anything fit to eat. There's the wine, of course. And books. But old William never had more than a quarter of my scholars, and he lived like a bishop, before he was one."

"It is that locust you have. And you are like enough to have less, now that Guibert has fallen in with Bele Alys."

"Bele Alys? I thought she was out of a song."

"You would," said Gilles patiently. "And so she is. That song was made for her when she first came to Paris."

"It's a good tune," said Abelard. "*Main se leva Bele Alys*"—he stopped his humming abruptly. "I wonder—but it could hardly have been."

"What?"

"About two weeks ago I was looking out one night,

late. And I saw two in the shadow at the steps. I did not know they were living creatures till they moved, and the moon shone on her face. And then they came together again, and—" He hesitated, but the silence into which he spoke accepted him. "It seemed to me, watching them, as if they made all the things that we contend for, nothing. And then it struck for midnight, and the woman darted away like a swallow, and who was it but that lank cat of a Guibert sidling across the square."

"And so you mocked him?"

"And myself too."

"You need not have done that," said Gilles, "if the woman was Bele Alys."

"A scullion and a harlot," said Abelard bitterly. "And for a while—"

"Well?"

"It seemed to me as though . . . as though they had immortality."

"And so they had. Do you remember Boethius' definition of eternity, 'to hold and possess the whole fullness of life in one moment, here and now, past and present and to come'? That is what Bele Alys gives to a man when he takes her in his arms. Until she wearies."

Abelard listened, bemused. "Gilles," he said suddenly, "I do not believe a word of it. It is you who are the sorcerer. There is no woman living could give a man that."

"Bele Alys has, to many men," said Gilles soberly. "Though not all of them, perhaps, have recalled it in the language of Boethius. But—man, you saw it for yourself."

"Not with that hound," said Abelard obstinately.

"It is grace, not merit," said Gilles gravely. "Yet another point in which she has something of the divine nature. She will sell herself, when she chooses, for a king's ransom—if she wants the money: and she will give herself, when she chooses, for charity. Like enough, your mongrel looked up at her with the eyes haunting out of that scraped face of his—"

"Don't I know it?" said Abelard. "The drunken, lecherous hound. But he can sit in the corner mouthing that flute of his with those eyes gazing at you over it and the tune plucking at you like a hand in your breast, till I have hurled things at him. It's either that, or throw back your head and howl like a dog yourself."

"Blessed are the poor in spirit," said Gilles drily. "Well, she will soon weary of him. But meantime, look to your purse."

Abelard shrugged. "Most of the year's fees are gone already," he said bitterly. "Now that I think of it, I have half a mind to go for the summer back to Brittany."

Gilles sat silent, his mouth pursed, frowning to himself. Still frowning, he rose, and went to sit down in his familiar chair beside the hearth. When he spoke, it was as a man who has come to a decision and does not know whether or not he mislikes it.

"Fulbert," he said harshly, "is wishful that you should give up your separate lodging and live with him. He bade me say that he has room for Guibert also, for he knows that you must have a man about you, and his old Grizzel, though bearded, is a woman, and enough to do in the kitchen. So that you will still have Guibert to fetch and carry for you, but no outgoings of money nor false marketing." He talked on, as if not to observe the rigor that had crept on the younger man's face. "There is a great room that looks to the Seine near the top of the house; it is draughty with windows, but there would be room for yourself and your books. He does not any more climb so high, with the stiffness of his knees."

He ceased speaking and the air was rigid with silence. At last Abelard spoke.

"Why has he done this?"

"He would take you for the half of what your separate housekeeping costs you now. But he asks you, with diffidence, if in part consideration of your board and lodging, you would, in such leisure as your weightier studies afford you, instruct his niece. He is ambitious for her, as you have yourself perceived. He bade me say that she will be at your disposal at any hour you choose." Gilles's voice rasped like a saw.

Abelard sat grimly silent. Suddenly he rose, and coming down the room, stood square in front of Gilles. "Is the man right in his wits?"

"I thought it my duty," said Gilles deliberately, "to point out to him that his niece was seventeen and you as yet only in your thirty-seventh year. But he spoke much of your reputation for chastity, and of St. Jerome and his pupil Eustochium, and also of Origen. He seemed to me imperfectly acquainted with the circumstances of that Father."

Abelard laughed shortly. He had begun tramping up and down the room. Gilles had turned his back on him and was looking into the empty hearth, but a muscle in his cheek twitched with irritation each time Abelard passed.

The tramping ceased. Abelard drew out a stool from

the chimney corner, and sat down, leaning forward, his elbows on his knees.

"Gilles," he said, and the old man stirred wretchedly, for the voice was suddenly a boy's voice, uncertain of himself. "Tell me. Is it to be Yes or No?"

Gilles lifted his hand and dropped it wearily. "I am no man to ask that question of, Peter," he said slowly. "For never in my life have I said No to a thing I greatly desired."

The tension had lessened. Abelard sat back, hugging his knees.

"Odd," said he, "but do you know, Gilles, I do not think I have, either. Only," he went on slowly, like a boy analyzing himself for the first time, "I have wanted so few things."

Gilles stirred in relief. He turned to Abelard, the old speculative light in his eye. "I have sometimes wondered, Peter, what were the things you did want."

Abelard sat, his brows knit. "I believe," he said slowly, "I believe the thing I have most wanted all my life was to be free. I think perhaps that was one reason why I told my father I did not want to go and be squire at Clisson, and be knighted, and that Guillaume might go instead."

"It was a strange thing that your father gave consent," said Gilles. "But he was not like other men, ever."

Abelard's eyes had softened. "He was more of a saint than any man I ever knew," he said eagerly. "And he would have been a rare scholar, if there had been any schooling in his youth. I have seen him listen when Guillaume and I were at our lessons. I have thought that was why he was willing I should go to the schools,

[33]

for his own heart lay there, and it was as though he satisfied himself in me. Only, he would have gone to the cloister, in my place, I think. You know, he has gone there, now."

Gilles nodded. "I rode with him once, years ago. He was a young man then, and I not so much older. And even then I noted that at every crucifix he did not pass with a reverence, as the rest of us might, but got off his horse and knelt, and I could see his lips move. I asked him what the words were that he said, but it was a long time before he would tell me."

"What was it?"

"*Thy cross I adore. I call to mind Thy passion. Thou who didst die for the sins of the world, have mercy upon us.*"

Reluctantly as Gilles spoke, the words made a curious silence about them, alien in that place. Abelard sat biting his under-lip. Gilles was the first to speak. "It was men like your father," he said, "who made the liturgies."

Abelard looked up, again eager for speech. "I never had a hard word from him, all my life," he said. "It was my mother who gave us whatever chiding we got. And that was little enough."

"She was a Quelhac," said Gilles. "I saw her when she was a little girl: with great eyes, as wild as a hare."

"She has them still," said Abelard. "But I sometimes think she is happier now than in all the years. You know, she took the veil at Poitiers two months after my father entered at Saint Savin. It was as though they both had a vocation, a kind of spring in their hearts. And now their peace flows like a river. It is not the worst end, Gilles, to have served in the wars and taken a wife and begotten

[34]

children and looked to one's lands, and then at the last
take down one's sail and ride at anchor in God."

"Would it have contented you?"

Abelard got restlessly to his feet. "I hate to be tied."

"You know what they called you at Laon?" said Gilles.
"*The masterless man.* Why do you make such enemies,
Peter? You might as well have sat out your time at old
Anselm's feet, and been received by him as *magister.*
Now they all say that you teach, never having been
taught yourself. Use authority, and rebel when you are
Authority yourself. It wastes time else."

"I could not endure it," said Abelard, frowning. "Anselm didn't know anything. None of them do. At least,
they know, but they don't understand anything. They
swallow, but they don't chew."

"The sincere milk of the Word," said Gilles solemnly.

Abelard groaned. "Do you remember," he said suddenly, "what Augustine said, that a man should serve the
understanding of things? I shall be content if when I
am dead someone says that about me. And that is why
they like me, Gilles, these youngsters. There is a natural
reasonable soul in most things, when they're young."

"I doubt it," said Gilles. "Yet it may be even a hen
when it is young thinks it may some day fly like a hawk.
Then it grows up, and squawks when it sees one. They
are beginning to squawk, Peter."

"Let them," said Abelard. He straightened his shoulders. "I can do what I please with the young men anyhow."

"Freedom for yourself," said Gilles reflectively. "And
power of life and death over everybody else. Well, it is
the nature of eagles—and hawks. But tell me, Abelard,

[35]

have you never in all your life wanted anything else?"

Abelard stopped in his restless stride. "There was one time," he said, "but it was only when I was tired. It was after that terrific fight with William of Champeaux, the time I had my schools at Corbeil. And suddenly my head stopped thinking. There was nothing I cared about. And I went back to Le Palais, to Denise."

"Denise?"

"My little sister. She was the youngest. There was myself, and Guillaume, and Raoul, and Dagobert, and Denise. I think maybe Denise came off worst, with having a saint for a father. He did betroth her when she was nine to a Montreuil-Bellay, but the boy died of measles when he was sixteen, and things drifted. And I was away, and they two, Berengar and my mother, did not think how time went. And when they did, she had set her heart, and more than that, on Hugh the Stranger—a landless squire my father had—and they let her have him. He was steward for my father. And they live there, Hugh and Denise, still. You see, Guillaume married a Clisson, and Le Palais is a little fief beside hers. So Hugh farms the land for Guillaume, and there's a bunch of children with soft heads and round eyes bustling about the orchard, like chickens. Denise is like an apple tree when the sun has been on it; you put your hand on her and you can feel the kindness of the earth. And I was as weak as a cat. I used to lie on the grass that summer, no feeling in me at all. I could not read two lines without going dizzy. And I felt that I would have given all I had to be like Hugh and sweat all the mischief out of me at the hay, and come back and lie with something soft and kind like Denise all night. And I could have cursed my

[36]

wits that had spoiled me for living, and then left me drained like a piece of tripe. And my head—God, how it ached! And then Denise used to come—there weren't any children then, but she was carrying her first, and she would sit beside me on the grass for hours and hold my head in her two hands—"

Gilles raised his head. "Ah, those two hands," he cried, and Abelard wondered at the sudden harshness of passion in his voice. "If only they knew it, it is not their beauty, it is that divine kindness they have. That moment when they take your head in their two hands and carry it to their breasts."

Abelard stood still. "No woman," he said, very low, "has ever done that to me." He stood for a moment looking at the old man, sunk in his chair, and then walked over to the door.

"You may tell Fulbert it is Yes," he said quietly, and went out.

CHAPTER V

Domine, probasti me—O Lord, thou hast searched me and known me; thou knowest my downsitting and mine uprising: thou understandest my thought afar off. Gilles's voice fell silent, and his eye left the Psalter to rest on the still bar of sunlight that turned the oak of the floor to massy gold. It was the 28th of September, and not yet six o'clock: outside there was no sound but the intermittent drone of the pigeons, persistent and belated lovers. For weeks the sun had risen and set in unfathomable cloudless blue: there was warmth even in the starlight. All September the Ile de Cité had lain in a trance of heat, yet not the lifeless heat of August: there was a shiver of expectation in the early mornings, exhilaration in the heavy evening dews. Like these two, thought Gilles. Never had he seen love so still, or so aware.

Yet not the stillness of possession. Of that, old and wise lover as he was, Gilles was sure. These two were drenched with love, as the air is drenched with light. Even so a river runs, smoother and deeper, with no fleck or ripple upon it, before the waterfall: so arches a wave, green and crystalline, before the plunge and the smother of foam.

Had he, or had he not, willed that these two should come together? Or had some deeper purpose than his own moved him, half blind and half aware? Here it was, at any rate, before his eyes: the absolute of human passion. Prophets and kings had desired to see the thing that he saw, and had not been able. How indeed should it have befallen, unless with these? This man, to whom his heart had warmed in spite of himself, with the arrogant head and the clean lines marred by irritation and by sleepless nights, and the intelligence that would reach down a handful of stars from heaven and set them by his book to read by: the hawk had become an eagle, a golden eagle flying to the sun. Two days ago he had spoken to his young men, already crowding Paris for the autumn session: "I said, ye are gods." Young Pierre de Montboissier had come to Gilles after it, almost hysterical with rapture, till Gilles sobered him by setting him to a copy of Latin verses. Gilles's eyes twinkled as he remembered them.

THE CLOISTER OF NOTRE DAME

"The Socrates of Gaul, great Plato of the West,
Of all the ancient Masters of the Word
The peer, or greater: prince of human knowledge,
Our Aristotle—"

"Short of making him Chief of the Squadron of the Prince-Archangels," Gilles had amiably commented, "I do not see that you could have said much more." And when Pierre reddened and made to throw them into the fire, "Keep them, my son. It was Judas who gibed at the alabaster box. Keep them. They'll serve you some day—*absit omen*—for his epitaph."

And Heloise? Gilles put his hand across his eyes. Fragments floated through his mind, broken metaphors. "And I John saw the holy city . . . her light like unto a stone most precious, clear as crystal." Mere breath of flutes at eve, he had called her, and if the breathing of pipes could fashion a girl, as the word of God fashioned the world, it would be such as she. Evening dew he had thought her, but it was dew of the morning now, crystal, but with the fire of the sunrise in it. There were times that he hardly dare touch her hand: and other times when he sat watching her, marveling what manner of man the other must be, that he could so long forbear.

"And the beast went timidly, for awe of the goddess," he had once muttered to himself: and Heloise, sitting reading on her stool at his feet, had lifted her head.

"What beast?"

Gilles laughed a little. "I was wondering," he said, "how it comes that men love to postpone delight: but women never."

"And you think?"

[39]

"I think it is because men live in their imagination as well as in their senses." He paused.

"And women only in their senses?" Heloise's voice was small and cold.

Gilles laughed softly and touched the plait of hair with one finger.

"Does it anger you to be in this, as in all things, the exception, Heloise?"

Heloise pondered. "I think," she said slowly, "it frightens me, when men think about women as you do. For it might come—it is bound to come—that one would be no more Heloise but just a woman, and then—"

Gilles raised his hand to stop her. "Child," he said hurriedly, "it is not canny to be so wise."

"It is wisdom, then?" The eyes that had hoped for contradiction darkened.

Gilles did not speak. His eyes were on her face, but she could see in them that he was working out a thought beyond her.

"I have sometimes thought," he said at last, "that this is the difference between loveliness and beauty. Wisdom, the knowledge of things past, the memory of the tree in Eden. Loveliness is an easy thing, an apple tree in blossom, and most women have something of it, in their youth. But beauty—one or perhaps two, in every generation. Persephone come back from the dead, with the knowledge of the kingdoms of it in her face."

"And are they happy?" Her eyes clung to his.

Gilles sat up with a sudden violence almost as of anger. "Happy? What do they want with happiness? They know ecstasy. Happiness? A dog asleep in the sun."

He had turned away from her in his sudden fear. There

was no sound from her, and when he turned to her, his heart stood still at the look on her face. "They know ecstasy," but what was in the words to bring transfiguration? A moment later, and his duller ear had caught the sound of Abelard's foot on the stair.

Gilles sighed and turned again to his book. "*Thou compassest my path and my lying down, and art acquainted with all my ways. For there is not a word in my tongue—*" The door latched open and Heloise came swiftly across the room, so swiftly that she was on the floor at his feet with her head in his lap before he could see her face. But he could feel her quivering.

"May God damn him," said Gilles to himself unreasonably. But he said nothing: only his hand fell on her shoulder and held it.

Heloise moved her head reassuringly against his knee. "Go on reading, Gilles," she said. "I like to hear it."

"*Whither shall I go from thy spirit? or whither shall I flee from thy presence? If I ascend up into Heaven, thou art there: if I make my bed in Hell, behold, thou art there. If I take the wings of the morning, and dwell in the uttermost parts of the sea; even there shall thy hand lead me, and thy right hand shall hold me.*"

With a little laugh Heloise slipped her head from under his hand, and looked up at him.

"Not much use in going away, then?" she said, half ruefully.

Gilles looked down at her. There was disquiet in her eyes, but no graver trouble. "Serve him right for a clumsy fool," he thought.

[41]

"Do you want to go away?"

"I must." She looked away from him. "Gilles, can you think of something? I want to go away. Before anybody knows."

"That is easy enough," said Gilles placidly. "It is the Eve of St. Michael. I shall send Jehan to Argenteuil with an offering for tomorrow's Feast, and greetings to my cousin the Abbess. Jehan is always glad of an excuse to go to Argenteuil, for his sister's son keeps the change-house at the ferry. It is a long time since you have seen the Sisters. You can ride pillion behind him, and come back with him this evening, or not, as you choose. Do you want to come back?"

"I do not know," said Heloise. She was twisting one of her plaits of hair in and out of her fingers. She looked up at him with a sudden burst of courage. "I don't know —until I have gone away. I want to think."

Gilles nodded. "Is your uncle at Mass?"

"He is."

"Then go back, and get your cloak and whatever gear you want, and leave word with your Grizzel that I am sending Jehan to Argenteuil, and he must go at once. Fulbert will come to ask me about it, and I shall tell him that I urged you to take the opportunity, and even to stay a while, for you have kept close at your books all summer, and my cousin at Argenteuil is aggrieved that you have neglected them for so long. Truth has as many coats as an onion," he added reflectively, "and each one of them hollow when you peel it off."

Heloise had risen while he was speaking: she stooped and held his hand against her cheek.

[42]

"And send Jehan to me as you go out," concluded Gilles. "He'll likely be in the stable."

"I'll find him," said Heloise joyfully, and went out.

It was still before seven when they rode across the Grand Pont to the north bank. Passing the Schools, Heloise had pulled her hood over her face. The windows were open, and on the sills and even on the stairs leading up to the open door the young men were thick as bees. They were intent as she went by, and the deep voice from within rang with a curious solemnity through the arches. There came a quick roar of laughter, and the men outside plucked at the gowns of those on the window-sills to hear the joke, and one slid off and fell almost under the feet of Jehan's mare, looking up and still laughing. There was a market on the Grand Pont, and they had to go slowly: but once across the bridge, Heloise threw back her hood. The air was cooler than it had been for weeks, and there was a ripple and stray windflaws on the Seine, and moving golden lights on the walls of the Port St. Landry as the boats for the market made waves alongside it. Jehan was silent, but there was comfort in the lee of the solid back. He would likely not say a word till he got off to dismount her at the ferry at Asnières: the mare jogged easily, and Heloise sat in a kind of remote peace that was not unpleasant.

She need not think yet. The gray mood of fear that she had wakened with at dawn had gone. She had wakened early often enough at Argenteuil, but dawn in Paris was a horrible thing. She had opened her window and leaned out in the dread blue light that comes before the first streak in the east, and the city and the river both

seemed dead, and both stank, a cold stench, as of ashes
and foul water. She had gone to bed dizzy and flaming
with his kisses: he had half carried her up the stairs to
her room, and standing on the threshold, loath to let her
go, he had taken her in his arms again and kissed her,
more terribly for the silence they must keep. For many
nights he had done that, but suddenly last night he had
stood still and with his mouth just parted from hers he
had said, "Tomorrow night," and she shrank, and clung
to him the more desperately for her shrinking. If he had
taken her then before she had time to think, before that
evil dawn stood between her and his kisses. But what
would it have been like, then, to waken this morning?
Would she have seemed to herself as foul as the dead
street and the dead river? She had left the window and
crept back to bed and said her prayers over and over
with her face buried in the pillow, and then slept late,
and wakened only to hear him shouting up the stair to
Guibert to bring him the *Categories* instead of the *Ana-
lytics*. Guibert was a poor scholar, and she had run downstairs barefoot, with only her cloak about her, to help
him find it, and Abelard, coming up the stairs like the
North Wind, collided with Guibert at the turning, and
raising his head, saw her standing at the top. Guibert slid
like an eel between his master and the wall, and was gone.
Abelard stood still, staring up at her. She had never seen
desire naked, with no tenderness to mask it, and here as
well was something more terrifying than desire, a kind
of mastery. Her arm went suddenly across her eyes, and
when Abelard pulled himself together and called her a
casual greeting before he turned to follow Guibert, she
answered him barely audibly. Then she had dressed and

gone, hardly knowing what she would ask, to find Gilles.

And with Gilles it was peaceful and safe, and nothing mattered as much as she had thought it did. And she need not think until she reached Argenteuil, and not even then, for she need not come home tonight.

The ferry-boat was on the other side of the river when they came to Asnières, and no one about. Jehan put his hands round his mouth and shouted an "Ohé!" that made Heloise cover her ears. Three small urchins ran out of the ferry-man's hut, and ran in again shouting. The mother came, with her hand over her eyes, a small, red-haired woman, stood for a moment, and then came down to the boat, with the eldest urchin, and began rowing across. Meantime Jehan had dismounted Heloise, and stood holding the mare by the head.

"Where's your man?" said he, when the barge nosed the bank and swung round with the current. He stooped to hold her, and Heloise led the mare on board, reluctant and starting at the sound of her hooves on the wooden bottom. Then Jehan leaped on board, and the barge crept back, against the current this time: Jehan lifted another oar, and set to, with long steady sweeps.

"He's in his bed," said the woman briefly. "And if it hadn't been that I knew you, and knew you handy with the oar, you might have stayed and shouted your fill. For I can make shift to bring her across, but I can get her back, against the current, no way."

"It's changed days with you, my woman, that you couldn't get a man to help you," said Jehan, looking round at her with a slow twinkle.

"They're at the harvest," she said placidly. "They say the weather will break after the Feast. And there's not

so many come this way, since the killing in the woods
last May. Are you not feared yourselves?"

"Eudes isn't likely to touch a man of Notre Dame
again," said Jehan grimly.

The woman laughed. "He'd take Our Lady's self, if
he thought he could get her ransom," said she. "But God
help him, indeed he was drunk that day." The boat had
bumped the other bank, and Jehan made it fast and set
Heloise on shore.

"Would you have a drink of milk, mistress?" said the
woman kindly. "It's ill riding in the sun on an empty
belly. I was just stribbing the cow when I heard yon ox
bellowing, and she very near sent the milk over me at
the roars of him."

Jehan's stolid countenance mellowed into a broad grin.

"Indeed I was thirsty," said Heloise gratefully. She
followed the woman to the threshold of the hut, and out
from it came a scattering of hens and a sow grunting, the
smallest urchin pursuing with terrific zeal. She took the
wooden bowl, white with age and scrubbing, from the
woman's hand and drank, though the warmth of the milk
a little distressed her.

"Do you know," she said, "it is the same bowl that you
gave me a drink out of when I was little, and my uncle
was taking me to the Convent. It had the same chip out
of the rim, and I wanted to drink out of the chip, and
spilt the milk all down my dress, and my uncle scolded
me and I cried, and you wiped me up and scolded him
for scolding me. Do you remember?"

"She has scolded too many men since to have mind of
that," said Jehan.

"I mind it rightly," said the woman. "I was heart-vexed

[46]

for you that day. You had the saddest eyes I ever saw in a child's head. Were they good to you where you were going? Many a time I wondered."

"Good to her?" said Jehan. He swung Heloise to her pillion. "You'd have thought she was the one kitling with forty cats."

"Indeed it's true," said Heloise soberly. She was thinking, with a vague wonder at herself, how little they had been in her mind since.

"I was reared near Argenteuil," said the woman. "It's a heartsome place. They had my mother in at a feast time to help in the kitchen, and I would watch for her coming out, for she'd have the full of her petticoat of pieces of goose and cake and raisins and the like. They'd have taken me in the kitchen myself," she went on, her eyes on the dancing river that slipped past their feet. "And if I'd known what was good for me," with a sudden vindictive gleam at Jehan, "I'd have gone there and had no truck with the likes of him yonder."

"You've never had truck with me, yet," said Jehan gallantly, looking down at her from the saddle.

"Quit your loose talk before the young girl," said the ferry-wife righteously. She looked up at Heloise with a quick, shrewd kindliness. "If you knew as much about them as what I know, mistress," said she, "you'd stay where you're going. You'll be staying the night, itself?"

"I don't know," said Heloise. She felt her face redden, and was glad Jehan's back was towards her. "You see, Jehan must come back this evening."

"And by the same token," said Jehan, suddenly serious, "if you can't make shift to get the ferry back from the

[47]

far side, I'll set the young mistress and the mare across, and bring it back myself."

"And then swim?" said the ferry-wife. "You're the first man I ever knew handy about a boat that could."

Jehan's face fell and he swore softly. "That means the other road," he said, "by St. Denis. And as far again. We'll need to be leaving before Vespers, mistress."

"You'll have about got there by then if you hurry the way you're doing," said the ferry-wife with gravity. She took the coins that Jehan reached down to her for their passage, and looked up at him with merry creases puckered about her eyes, a kind of elfin mischief that made Heloise ponder. There was small beauty about her, and she looked, if anything, older than Jehan, and yet Jehan rode jauntily for a while, and even whistled. Then the shadow of the woods fell on them, and the mare's hooves went softly on the pine-needles, and the air droned with the cooing of the doves that gave the wood its name, and Heloise rode, drugged with the sweetness of the day.

✦

The bell above the chapel tinkled for Nones. It was barely three o'clock, but the tinkling was persistent and lasted long, for the sisters slept in the cool dorter between dinner and Nones, and on drowsy afternoons were hard to waken. Heloise had gone to the cloister after dinner, protesting that she was not tired, and had promised Godric to copy a page from the book of Alcuin's letters that the Abbot of Corbei had lent. Now at the first tinkle of the bell she fled down the pleached walk, through the kitchen garden and the orchard, to the bees' garden under

the southern wall. The river ran beneath it on the outer
side: that wall was the oldest thing in the Convent, for
Charlemagne built well. The terrace on the inner side was
smooth with grass, white now after the long drought of
the summer, but short and soft and thick; and below it
stood the beehives, protected from the rest of the orchard
by a great box-hedge. The flowers in the bees' garden
were most of them over: but the bees were away all day
in the heather and the fading gorse of the bog country
that lay league after sunny league by the western-flowing
Seine.

There was a little arbor cut in the boxwood, and in a
rough wooden shrine like a dovecote a small companionable Virgin suckled her child. Heloise knelt for an Ave
to the archaic friendly countenance, and sat down on the
grass at her feet. The September sun slept on the wall,
and the boxwood breathed that old kind smell which
must, thought Heloise, be the oldest thing in the world,
so secret is it and so wise; and from the manuscript on
her lap came that other ancient smell, of vellum that men's
hands have handled. Three hundred years, the abbot had
said.

She turned the pages, reading here and there. "*I have
laid aside the pastoral care, and now sit quiet at St. Martin's, waiting for the knocking at the gate. . . . Send me
a sheepskin for the winter, white if you can, for the
white has the best wool.*" So old and so holy, and yet
knowing how cold the winter would be on his old
withered arms and thin body. "*The time draws nigh
when I must leave this hospice of the body, and go out
to things unknown.*" Then even the Blessed Alcuin did
not know?

PETER ABELARD

"Beside the margin of the white-winged sea
I wait the coming of the silent dawn."

She halted at that, the compassion of youth for remote
old age turned into quick reverence: and as if the change
in her mood had power on the chance phrases that met
her eye, she read with growing wonder.

"*O my beloved, remember me. I shall be yours in life
or in death. . . . And even if some other place is destined
to hold my body, yet I think that my soul shall find its
rest with you. And though diversity of merit shall have
one live more blessed than another, yet the equality of
eternity shall have them all live happy. As one sun shines
on all, yet is seen more clearly by some eyes than by
others, so shall the kingdom of heaven be. . . . This is
the blessedness of the life hereafter, that that never is
absent which always is beloved. I have spoken too much,
but who knows whether it will be given me to write tomorrow, or whether you and I, after tomorrow, will ever
hold sweet converse again?*"

She turned the pages more hurriedly: this old voice
from a forgotten world had too much power. This was
better: Gilles would like it. "*Here is an old man weak in
the wits asked to scrutinize Heaven, who hath not yet
learned the ordinary ways of earth, and to expound the
vagabond courses of the wandering stars, who never yet
was able to understand the nature of grass that grew.*"
And this—"*The origin of evil is the loss of good.*" That
was for— She turned the page resolutely. "To a friend
minded to take monastic vows." Alcuin, she remembered,
had died Abbot of St. Martin at Tours, yet most of his
life had lived a simple deacon. "*Remember that in any
place where a good many men are living together, good*

*and evil are found. . . . If place could help, never had
angels fallen from Heaven, nor man sinned in Paradise.
A wise mind keeps its own mastery. There is in men a
royal mind—"* She closed her eyes. She could fly no
further. At every turn she found him. *Mens regalis:* it
was the living image of the man she loved.

She was going back. Had she not known all along
that she was going back? The apathy of the long sunlit
ride had stayed with her through the wood, and the
second crossing at the ferry beyond Colombes, and up
the cobbled street of Argenteuil, and even while they
dismounted and Jehan knocked at the familiar gate. Then
the broad beaming face of Soeur Laure the portress
looked through the grille, and with many exclamations
Heloise was drawn in. Jehan set down his load and made
his excuses: he was for seeing his sister's son and was off,
panting for a drink.

"Little one, little one, you're white," said the portress.
She set Heloise down on the bench. "Sit still, child, and
I'll bring you a drink of water. It's the long ride in the
sun."

"I just turned dizzy for a minute," said Heloise. "If I
might lie on the bench—" She slipped face downwards,
her arms about her head, and lay there listening to the
hurried slapping of Soeur Laure's wide shoes down the
flagged path to the well. It was not the ride in the sun.
It was this shut-in place. She was going back. If she could,
she would start on her own feet now, before ever Soeur
Laure came back. Her body had known it before her
mind, had known it at the first smell of the dark little
room, the faint perpetual frowsiness of unwashed rags,
for the beggars came here and sat till the almoner could

see them, and mingling with it the half-sweet, half-sickly
scent of the bunch of herbs, dried thyme and rosemary,
that hung from the middle of the ceiling, black now with
flies. Deadly nausea had come upon her, and for a moment
the room went black. But she must be wise. She must
live the day through, and talk and smile, and by that
blessed chance they must start early, because of the long
way round by St. Denis. Her heart sang as she remembered it.

The well-rope was creaking, the old familiar creak.
Heloise rose and went down the path. She was smiling
now.

"It was so hot," she said. "Let me just drink from the
dipper." She knelt on the mossy stone and drank thirstily;
then, in spite of Soeur Laure's predictions on the risk of
it after being overheated, she splashed the water in the
bucket over her face and arms, drawing up her wide
sleeves to the shoulder. Soeur Laure looked kindly at the
young slenderness of them.

"You're thriven, little one," she said. "They are nothing
like the sticks they were."

Heloise sat back on her heels, laughing, shaking the
water from her fingers. Soeur Laure emptied the water
that was left into the little stone runnel that ran through
the garden in the outer court, and swung back the bucket.
The drops from the bottom edge fell a long way into
the darkness. Heloise could hear the faint chime of them,
very far and sweet.

"Do you remember, Sister," said she, "how I used to
come and torment you when I was little, for drinks? And
all the while it was only to hear that noise."

"I couldn't think," said Soeur Laure, "how on earth

so thin a child could hold all the water you drank. But it was maybe that that gave you your clear skin."

"It's better water here than in Paris," said Heloise. "You daren't drink it there."

"And how's your good uncle?" said the portress. "And Master Gilles?"

"They're both well. Uncle is thinner, I think, but he says it is the dry weather has dried him up."

"It would take more than this summer to dry up Master Gilles, I warrant," said the portress, chuckling, "or Reverend Mother, either. But there, I hear them. She'll be scolding me for chattering," and the wide skirts bustled back to the lodge.

A very deep, very musical voice came through the open chapter-house window. *"Now to God the Father, God the Son . . ."*

"Amen."

Chapter was over. The door into the outer court opened, and the Abbess came through, a short woman, massive as Gilles but without his height, singularly fresh and fair in spite of the folds of fat, the same shrewd, small eyes, but with points of steel in them, Heloise felt, for the kindly candle-flame in Gilles's.

Heloise went a few steps to meet her, halted, and then slipped on her knees to kiss the Abbess's ring.

"Child," said the deep voice, "you are a sight for sore eyes. I was for giving you a good scolding, but I have no mind to it now. How did you come?"

"I rode behind Jehan. Your cousin, Master Gilles, was sending him with offerings for the Feast tomorrow, and he—I begged to come too."

"And where is Jehan?"

"He went to see his sister's son. But he set the saddle-bags down in the lodge. And of the wine, Master Gilles bade me say that he would gladly have come to sample it with you himself, but that you will please to pledge him, and that he has added the extra bottle that he would undoubtedly have drunk."

The Abbess chuckled. "Gilles and I had always a like taste in wine. But it was a risk to send it in this heat. I must have it down to the cellar straight." She lifted her white fingers in dismissal—the hands so like and yet so unlike Gilles's, for these were dimpled and plump and a huge sapphire blazed on one—and turned to the portress's lodge. In a flash the other nuns, hanging discreetly back while the Abbess talked, were crowding round Heloise.

"Little one, little one, how you are grown! Have you come to stay? Is it true that Master Peter Abelard says you are the best scholar he has ever had? Is that the way they wear their hair now? And what has kept you all this while? Oh, Heloise, it has been so dull since you went away!"

Heloise was passed from hand to hand, breathless and affectionate, and in her heart so far off. Did they notice nothing? Did they not know it was a kind of gargoyle that was grinning at them and making agreeable noises? Why had she come? She greeted the last, and then looked round her, suddenly grave.

"Where is Soeur Godric?"

"Didn't you hear about it? She missed the corner step, coming down from the choir—you know how dark it is—and broke her leg. And it isn't knitting very well, for they say she is too old. So she is in the infirmary now.

And Soeur Gisela is mistress of the novices. And Reverend Mother—"

There fell a silence, as the Abbess appeared in the doorway of the lodge.

"Now, now," said she. "That is enough chatter for a while. You can have Heloise after dinner, before you go to the dorter. Heloise, go and see Soeur Godric."

It was like the scattering of a flock of sparrows. Heloise watched the bowed heads and the meek shoulders disappear, heard the feet in the wide shoes shuffle down the cloisters. Could one have any pride in one's body if one hid one's feet in shoes like those? She crossed the court to the door beside the chapel, her head a little higher than its wont, in unconscious protest against those meek shoulders and against the secret fear in her own heart. She did not—she hesitated over the word—esteem Reverend Mother, but she respected her. It was not virtue, it was a kind of native hardihood, with all the self-indulgence. Was that first Abbess of Argenteuil, Charlemagne's daughter by Fastrada, like that; whelp of the tigress and the lion? She passed the chapel door, and paused. Poor Guibert, he had asked her to burn a candle for him, he did not say for what, and had given her two *sous* for a big one. Perhaps the sacristan would still be about, and she could buy it and set it alight at once, before it slipped her memory. She passed in, and the curious oppression that had almost stopped her heart in the lodge crept over her again. Yet this time not so purely physical; a bodily memory of restraint along with a mental embarrassment, a kind of hollowness in herself, a struggle to feel something that she had felt elsewhere, but never here. Once in Chartres, she remembered. She had asked Gilles why

Chartres had that strange compulsion, as though one's
body worshiped, even before one's mind did: and he
said that it had always been a sacred place, even among
the Druids, that most of its Bishops had been holy men,
above all St. Fulbert, who had built the Cathedral, and
that the very streets were full of his presence still. Heloise
had pondered: could the living and dying even of a holy
man be remembered by arch and stone? Gilles had
shrugged his shoulders.

"The habitation of God is with men," he said briefly.
"And perhaps it is easier for a hard heart to quicken
where one man has"—he hesitated—"apprehended God."

If that were so, then neither Fastrada's daughter nor
Reverend Mother was likely to leave that quickening.
But this was spiteful. It was herself who was hard of
heart. She lit Guibert's candle, crossed herself, and came
quickly out.

The infirmary was beyond the kitchen, and looked
south. Sitting up in bed was a tiny bent figure, bowed
over a kind of rude reading-desk. It looked up as the
door opened, peering short-sightedly, as old and wrinkled
and wise as a toad, with the same brilliant eyes. Heloise
dropped on her knees beside the bed, and caught the
meager hand.

"Well, well," said the toad.

"Oh, my dear," said Heloise remorsefully. "And you
are so thin. I think a lark would have legs like your
wrists."

"I know," said Godric comfortably. "Like the chicken-
bone the little boy held out to the witch. Short-sighted
she was, just like me. My dear, I would not mind the

legs going from me, if the eyes weren't too. But it was Providence sent you this day. Look at this," she pushed across the book over which she had been poring, a small quarto, stamped with the arms of Corbei. "Most of it is in a good hand, but at the last—"

"They have crowded it to get it all in," said Heloise. Godric was like Gilles, in that quick escape from personal relations into clear dry air. She looked at the page where Godric had been reading. *"Be careful in Italy when and where and how you eat, for Italy is a sickly country. Ah, but they were good days, when you and I sat quiet among the bookshelves."* She stopped, her eyes stinging in a quick surge of sorrow for the lonely patience of the old. Godric's mouth was quivering, but it widened into a crooked smile.

"We're all like that, the old hens," said she. "But tell me, Heloise, is it true that Master Peter says you are the best scholar he ever had?"

Heloise flushed. "It was a joke," she said. Why must she go scarlet at the naming of his name? Godric would take it for diffidence: Reverend Mother would not. "He said it to my uncle at supper one night, for fun. But you know what my uncle is like. He told everybody as if it were true."

Godric nodded.

"But he did say to Gilles de Vannes," went on Heloise manfully, "that I was the best-trained scholar he had ever had. And Gilles said he could well believe it, for the teacher who trained me was you."

"Orgulous as a peacock," said Godric. "That is what I shall be from this day. You have put another ten years on me in Purgatory. But what I want you to find is a different letter, to Argentueil. Not from Alcuin. The Abbot of Corbei said there was one, written to Charlemagne's daughter when she came here as Abbess, by Dungal."

"Dungal? It is a strange name," said Heloise.

"It's common enough where I come from, in Donegal," said Godric. "And he was an Irishman too. There's a worse crowded page than that. It may be on it. Look at the very end."

The infirmarian came in, looking a little scared. "Reverend Mother wants to know if you have the accounts ready, Godric, for she will be seeing the Steward this evening after Vespers."

Godric made a face like a wicked little boy. "Tell Reverend Mother," she said firmly, "that the sum for wine for the altar seems to me excessive and that I must look into it. But that she will have them by Nones."

The infirmarian went out, with small assurance. Godric looked at Heloise, the corners of her wide mouth pulled down. "It was the book from Corbei—I clean forgot. Bring me that book from the window, child. I have them copied, but not checked."

"Let's do it together," said Heloise. She laughed a little. "It is the one thing Master Peter is not good at," she said, and the softness in her voice would have betrayed her to a quicker ear. "He can't add."

"I am not very good at it myself," said Godric sadly.

"You read them out," said Heloise, slipping her tablets from her girdle, "and I'll put the figures down and add them."

Godric gruntled contentedly.

"To cakes for St. Martin's and fresh herrings . . . xxxv s.
To wine bought before Easter . . . . LXV s.
To outlay for the archdeacon in wine and fish . . . xx s. ivd.
To xxviii quarts and a pint from Perrot Lachose for
   the Feast of St. Aubin . . . . xv s.
To xxxiiii cheeses bought at Pons . . . . . . ix s.
To xii pairs of shoes for the poor on Holy Thursday xv s. 6d.
To herrings, eggs and mustard pepper and other small
   things . . . . xxv s."

Godric looked up. "There's the bell for Sext," said she.
"You must go to chapel. Do you think, child, you could
make out that letter for me and copy it, this afternoon,
maybe, when they're all asleep? I can easily make shift
to finish these myself. You'll find a blank page at the back
of the Blessed Gregory's Dialogues. Reverend Mother
will buy no more parchment. And indeed my hands are
so twisted I would only spoil it if I had it. But leave it
with me now."

At the door the girl turned for a last look. Godric
was stooped again above the Corbei manuscript, indomitable and solitary.

Heloise wakened with a start. She had fallen asleep,
her head resting against the wooden shrine. It was darker
than it had been, and she sprang to her feet in sudden
panic, lest Jehan should have come, and gone without
her. But it was only the haze above the river. The sun
was still high, and she sat down again with a breath of
relief. The book had fallen face downwards on the grass.
She picked it up guiltily, and smoothed the crumpled
page. "*We keep the hour of Sext*," she read, "*because at
that time they crucified Him, and there was darkness*

over all the land. . . . Of Vespers, propter Recessum Dei, *because of the departing of God: and because at evening the Lord was made known in the breaking of bread."*

Recessum Dei. The afternoon had grown closer and yet more still; so still that the running of the river outside the wall was audible. It was like the noise Time might make, if one could hear it slipping away.

Recessum Dei, the departing of God. Heloise stirred uneasily, and looked up at the rough little Virgin suckling her child. It was very old, she knew; the face was almost square, and out of all proportion with the body. The hands were large, and the feet were hidden. Then came to her mind the memory of the broken marble foot that Gilles had in his chest. He had found it when he was a young man ferreting for rabbits among the gorse on Montmartre. There used to be a temple there to Mars, said Gilles, "and his goddess walked there in the early morning barefoot through the wet grass." Abelard that morning had looked at her bare feet. She buried her face in the grass with a half-articulate cry. She had shivered when she saw his eyes that morning, and put her arm across her face. She was shivering now, but not with fear. *"Perfect love,"* the words that she had copied in the cloister that afternoon began rippling before her eyes, *"casteth out fear. Wherefore—"* she tried to halt them, for this was blasphemy, but the inexorable script ran on, *"I beseech you that ye present your bodies a living sacrifice, holy, acceptable unto God, which is your reasonable service."* It was blasphemy, but her heart had risen to greet it. She had found her God. In him she lived and moved and had her being. He was the very firmament above her, the air she breathed. It was between her and

[60]

the others, though they could not see it, a wall of glass, so that their voices came muffled through. Go back? She had never left him.

It was after sunset when they rode through the gate on the Grand Pont: it was slow in closing that night, for there were many coming and going with Michaelmas tomorrow. Fulbert was lighting his candle, and turned a troubled face upon her as she came in.

"My dear," he said, "we had all given you up. I doubt you should not have gone away. Yes, yes, I know, my child, Gilles explained it all to me. But I fear Master Peter is greatly vexed, greatly vexed."

He looked at her, ingenuous and distressed.

"He came back after his lecture, for his dinner, you know, and missed you. And I told him all that Gilles had said, and made your excuses as well as I could. He asked would you be back for supper, and I said I thought you would. And we kept supper back. I did not like to tell him until then that you might be staying a few days. And he seemed put out, my dear, very much put out."

"I am sorry, uncle," said Heloise. "You see, Jehan had to come the long way home, by St. Denis, he could not get the ferry at Asnières."

"I am sure it was not your fault, my dear. And I'm glad, very glad, you came back. You know, it is a great thing for a great clerk like him to give his time as he does to a child like you, and you must remember that, my dear. It is no wonder he was put out. I think, child, you had better wait up for him, till he comes in, and make your peace with him tonight."

Is he gone out?"

"He went out, after supper. And indeed he took none. I don't know where he was going. He didn't say. You'll promise to wait up for him, my dear? You could get out your books, and make a show of studying, to please him."

"I'll go up at once, uncle," said Heloise. Her heart was shaking through her.

"God bless you, little one," said Fulbert. He walked across to his great bed, the candle a little unsteady in his hand. "Don't be frightened, little heart." He stood still, looking up at her. "You know he is quick, but he is soon cooled. Though indeed I was frightened myself."

She stooped to kiss him, and climbed the stairs to her own room. For the first time in the ignorance and humility of her youth she had begun to realize how her flight might have moved him. Her eyes were blazing into the steel of her mother's mirror as she sat unplaiting her long hair. For a moment she let the black river of it fall on either side of her face, then, frowning at her boldness, she plaited it again, and freshened her face in the gilly-flower water that Audere had taught her to make at the convent. Stepping quietly, she went down the stair, opened the door of his great room, and crossing it, sat down on the window-seat to watch. But she got out no books. It was not by books she must appease his anger. The word trembled through her, exultant and afraid.

*

Sunset found Abelard at the ferry at Asnières. He had come out to meet them, striding hard: he would not let himself think that she would not come. But at Asnières, where the road, not much more than a bridle-track, came out on the river, and he looked across to the ferry-man's hut, the dark forest behind it and the light already fading on the river, there was no hope in his heart. They would have been here long since if they had been coming that night; Jehan would never have left it so late as this. He stood, leaning against a tree, looking at the river, the dark blot of the ferry-boat moored on the farther side. No living thing stirred. It had been a red sunset; it was glimmering on the boles of the pine trees, and on the parchment reeds across the river: the kind of sunset that made a man dream, not so much of a new Heaven as of a new earth, a turning of water into wine, of finer bread than can be made with wheat. And this night that was to have been his miracle, this night that he would have held all the sweetness of the world in his arms, this night that had set in upon the earth with such crimson pomp of light and mystery, was empty. She had left him, and had sent him no message, had written him no word.

He had been angry; but that was over now. He would be glad to be angry again. He had gone rigid with it, when old Fulbert told him first, stammering and repeating himself, and for a moment he had wondered if the old man had guessed and had packed her off to Argenteuil to secure her from him. But the agitation and distress of the good old soul were too genuine, and he had made a real effort to reassure him. Capricious was she, more practiced than he had thought, to tantalize him at the last? His lip curled, but in the same moment his heart reproached him. It could not be. His memory brought her back as he had that morning seen her, barefoot with only her cloak about her, flushed and childish from sleep: and the thought of it brought such a sharp anguish upon him that he all but groaned where he sat. Colic, he said to Fulbert, watching him with distressed eyes: one was apt to be disordered these September days: and Fulbert, much relieved at the turn of the conversation, continued in that vein till Abelard rose, saying he had a message for Gilles and must see him before his afternoon lecture. His mouth set as he strode down the cloister. How far was Gilles, ironic spectator of the foolishness of lovers, responsible for this?

Gilles sat hunched in his chair. By not so much as the flicker of an eyelid did he acknowledge Abelard's presence in the room. Abelard came and stood in front of him.

"Did you send Heloise to Argenteuil?"

"I did."

"Why?"

"Because she was eager to get away."

It was a blow between the eyes. Abelard stood silent, taking order with it.

"When did she come to you?"

"This morning, before seven. Her uncle was at Mass. You, I imagine, at your lecture."

"What did—" Abelard stopped. There were things he could not ask.

Gilles turned on him savagely. "She told me nothing. But she said that she wanted to get away—and quickly. That she must get away. She was shivering like a young sparrow on the ground. And I offered her Jehan's escort to Argenteuil, and bade her stay as long as she cared to, telling her I would make all right with her uncle. And if she stays there for good—" He stopped, softened in spite of himself by the misery on the younger man's face. Abe-

[64]

lard turned without a word and blundered to the door.

"Peter," called Gilles, suddenly relenting: but he was too late. He heard the heavy feet go down the stair.

He had known then that she would not come back, but he would not think. He had lectured in a kind of sullen fury: had come back to supper, listened to Fulbert's anxious twitterings in silence, eaten nothing, agreed with the old man that it was useless to expect her that night, and finally tramped downstairs and out of the house. Sit there he could not, and hear Fulbert rustling like a mouse until he went to bed. Guibert, about for once, was sitting mending his flute on the steps at the quay. He looked up, and a kind of timid understanding was in the dog-like eyes. Abelard cursed him. Had it come to this, that he was an object of pity to that water-rat?

"They will be late closing the gates tonight," volunteered Guibert nervously, "it being Michaelmas Eve. I heard Jehan say it when he was saddling."

Abelard flashed round. "Did you see him go?"

Guibert nodded. "I helped the young mistress mount. And Jehan said they were going and coming by Asnières, for it was the shorter road, so that they need not be leaving till after Vespers."

Abelard looked at him, transfigured.

"There's for a gaudy day tomorrow, Guibert," said he, and threw a silver piece into his lap.

But the exaltation had soon passed. With every bend of the road to Asnières, his eye scanned the lap of road in front of him: there were a few on foot, and most of them going the other way: a cart or two creaking home: but none riding. On and on he strode, with the sky and earth

[65]

a glory about him, his heart sick with hope: and now he stood there looking at the river.

The reeds that had been crimson paled to parchment again: the river flowed past, a small secret voice that seemed to grow louder as the light died from its surface. Abelard moved over to a balk of wood where they moored the boats, and sat there, his elbows on his knees, his hands clasped before him. It takes so short a while for light to go out. Only last night she was in his arms; and tonight the whole earth was empty. Back and forth went his mind on its ceaseless track. "A young sparrow on the ground—" Had he been rough with her, frightened her, his little one? It could not be that she would turn against all love for that. Or had her heart wakened and told her it was sin, and would she confess at Argenteuil and be held from him for ever? He could not think: his mind was too dazed and sore. He was past questioning the reason of her flight, or reasoning with his own blind anguish. She had left him. She was not coming back. Now and then the memory of her as he had seen her that morning came upon him with the same knife-thrust of desire: but something deeper in him bled continually.

The dull thud of oars on rowlocks came through the twilight; he raised his head and looked up the river. The boat came in sight, a broad-bottomed clumsy craft, heaped with barrels. The men at the oars looked like lay brothers, but the man at the tiller had a tonsure: he could see the light gleam on the shaven patch. At the same moment the steersman caught sight of the figure on the riverbank and recognized it. The oars halted, and the boat floated silently on.

"What brings you here so late, Master Peter?" Abelard

knew the voice, a decent grunting voice; Jean de Brosson, the cellarer from St. Germain.

"I walked farther than I thought," said Abelard, "and I was resting a while before I would go back."

Brosson wagged his head.

"Great clerk, little wit," said he. "Get in, Master Peter: we'll leave you as far as the bridge. And if you are too late for the gates, as I doubt you will be, there's always a bed for you at St. Germain."

Abelard hesitated, but the boat was already alongside, and Brosson's hand held out. It would be churlish to refuse; and there was comfort in the broad-beamed figure that had come upon him out of the loneliness of the night. He sat on a barrel behind Jean, and the boat swung again into midstream.

"Indeed we're full late ourselves," began Brosson, "but I was half the day arguing with yon baillie at Epinay. You know Epinay, this side of Argenteuil?"

"This side of Argenteuil?" said Abelard slowly. To say the name was a kind of bitter satisfaction to him. "I know Argenteuil."

"Well, you ask the Reverend Mother what she thinks of Pierre Quassart," said Brosson with relish. "One of their vineyards at Ormesson marches with . . ."

Abelard strove to listen, it would be some distraction from the gnawing in his heart, but will as he would, the voice evaded him, disjointed phrases catching up and making a teasing pattern on his brain. It was as though his mind came to the surface, and was beaten down again. They were past the ghostly army of the reeds. The woods were thick now on either side; they were going on for ever through a tunnel of dark trees, with this frog of Pharaoh giving voice' before him; an invisible frog only for the broad line of the back. Then the trees grew thinner, there was a kind of separateness in the light, as though the darkness disintegrated and fell away: and suddenly the moon rose above the heights of St. Cloud.

It lay before them, the valley of the Seine: at last, a great way off, the island with its towers. The moon rode high, intolerably lovely: some significance strained to him out of this silent aching beauty, and was pelted down by the rain of insignificant speech. Abelard could endure it no longer. He rose to his feet.

"Steady, man," said Brosson. "You'll have us all in the river."

"Could you set me ashore here?" said Abelard. "I have a chill on me, I think, with sitting yonder, and I should be glad to warm myself walking."

"It will be all hours before you get in," said Brosson solemnly. "You'd better sit where you are, and make sure of a drink and a warm bed with us at St. Germain. You'll never get past the gates tonight."

"They know me," said Abelard briefly. "I can get a drink at the *Deux Epées*. And I'd be better to warm myself with walking first."

Brosson, grumbling, turned the nose of the boat inshore.

"It's an ague, most like," said the man beside him, as they watched him go. "I could know him shivering."

"He is in poor case for walking, at that rate," said Brosson. "But, man, you couldn't turn him." He blew through his nostrils, and steered back into the current.

The relief of silence was so great that for a while Abelard walked, not happy, but with the lightness that

[68]

follows the loosening of a load. The remoteness of the moonlit world seemed to have softened his grief: he walked remembering, and remembering not her only, but a hundred things that they had read together, the strange starlight in her gray eyes when she was thinking, the queer blackness of them when he looked down at her after his kisses. "*Illam pulchritudinem aeternam quam amat et ad quam tendit omne quod amat.*" They had been reading John Scotus Erigena together. "That eternal Beauty which is beloved by, and towards which reacheth, whatsoever loveth." That was the first time he had held her in his arms. God knows it was of no set purpose, but at the "*ad quam tendit*" his hands had gone out in a sudden involuntary outthrust of longing, and had closed on hers. Oh, God!

He was near the Quartier now; late as it was, there was still light in the taverns. Not the *Deux Epées*, he decided: he would see too many that he knew. The *Ane Rayé* would be emptier, unless of shabby folk. They would let him across the bridge at any hour, and he must get the night spent in some fashion. He could not go back to that house. The inn garden stretched up the hill: indoors smelt stale and rank to him, coming in from the freshness of the autumn night, and some were at the raucous stage of drinking. It irked him to hear their solemn quarreling, and he took his bottle of Beaune and went out to one of the arbors under the vines. Farther up the garden he could hear low voices, and now and then a laugh that was smothered with a kiss, but he was beyond caring. Let them have their bliss.

The Beaune was good. He sat there, shivering no longer, listening vaguely to the noises of the September night. The quarrel indoors went on interminably: through it he could hear the quick rattle and the calling of the dice. Down in the Pré aux Clercs by the river they were dancing, and someone was playing the flute, with now and then a burst of singing. It came to him muffled, but gradually beat its way into his consciousness. He knew the tune, they used to dance to it at Nantes. He was too far off to hear the words, but the tune persisted in his brain, and he began humming it under his breath, his mind following it, idly seeking them. He had them now—

> Her mouth was cherry red beneath the tree
> —"Lady, for God, I now go over sea,
> For your hard heart that will not pity me"—

It had eluded him again. He listened, frowning in concentration: two more bars, and then the chorus swept up to him with a triumphant

> Et joie atent Gerars.

A good tune for him to be humming that night, but he was past irony. So might a man lie dying, he thought, waiting for the coldness to creep up past his knees, and hear the clatter of dishes and laughter in the room beyond, and neither curse nor bless.

> And joy awaits Gerars.

Strange, the effect of distance: let you be far enough away, and you heard only the infinite sorrowfulness of a crowd that is making merry, the inarticulateness of men that can wreak their hearts upon a single stave.

> Or a joie Gerars.

[70]

The song was ended. Joy hath now Gerars. Yet, though the voices had fallen silent, the flute played on. How was it that a flute can play no air but it makes it sorrowful? And here where a man had won his heart's desire, all the dumb longing of the groaning earth was in that final phrase.

A sudden harsher note jarred through the air. Someone, the man in the far arbor most like, had caught his hand in the strings of a bass-viol. Abelard moved restlessly on his bench. Flutes were sorrowful, but the strings —it was one's own nerves that the fingers plucked. A woman's voice spoke a word or two, persuading. Silence fell again. Then the hand began plucking, uncertainly, but even the discords were waking what had better be left asleep. There came half a dozen consecutive notes, the promise of a tune, curiously familiar, and suddenly a voice rose, challenging who would to listen, a glorious outrage on the moonlit peace.

> "So by my singing am I comforted
> Even as the swan by singing makes death sweet,
> For from my face is gone the wholesome red
> And sorrow in my heart is sunken deep.
>   For sorrow still increasing,
>   And travail unreleasing,
>   And strength from me fast flying
>   And I for sorrow dying,
> Dying, dying, dying,
> Since she I love cares nothing for my sighing."

The dicing had stopped: even the wranglers were silent. Abelard listened, indifferent and remote. Two weeks ago he had written that song, in some other life where he had thought that he knew the agony of love.

[71]

The unseen player plucked a single heavy note; his voice rose again, deeper and more resonant.

> "If she whom I desire would stoop to love me,
>   I should look down on Jove.
> If for one night my lady would lie by me,
> And I kiss the mouth I love,
>   Then come death unrelenting,
>   With quiet breath consenting,
>   I go forth unrepenting,
> Content, content, content,
> That such delight were ever to me lent."

Abelard had risen: he was shaking, gripping the table over which he leaned. The silence grew, as if desire itself were dumb. Then the unseen hands were plucking the strings, sharp tortured minors, intolerably sweet.

> "Innocent breasts, when I have looked upon them—"

Oh, God! Oh, God! Abelard stumbled out of the arbor and down the rough steps to the inn door, threw a handful of coins on the table, had a moment's glimpse of flickering candle-light and staring faces, and found himself out in the night. Swiftly and noisily as he went, the last words followed him, crying after him, beseeching him,

> "For her mouth, her mouth, her mouth,
> That on her beauty I might slake my drouth."

Two hours later, he came dragging down the Rue des Chantres, his shoulders bent and his eyes on the ground, making for home as blindly as a creature that the hounds have lost, but have hunted well-nigh to death. So tired was he, so broken, that he did not even raise his head to

see the candle-light in his high window, he had no heed
for the stumbling of his feet on the stair. She heard them,
those hopeless, dragging feet: it was her heart they
stumbled on, breaking with love and pity. He fumbled
at the latch, the door fell open: he came in a step or two
and stood, bewildered by the light: she saw his eyes seeking, not yet comprehending, suddenly wild with hope.
She was there at the window: he saw the small white
oval of her face, the black pools of her eyes. With a little
stifled cry, she held out her arms to him: he was on his
knees at her feet, his head buried in her lap, his whole
body shaking with a terrible tearless sobbing. Closer and
closer she held him, her master no longer, her lover
wounded to death. The sobbing ceased, but still he knelt,
his face pressed against her lap, his arms blindly clutching
her; now and then a long shudder quivered through him,
like a child worn out with crying. She stooped and took
his head and carried it to her breast.

CHAPTER VI

Put another log on the fire, Pierre," said Gilles. "It
is bitter cold. I have no great love for an early
Easter. The fast makes one feel the cold."

Pierre de Montboissier stooped to the pile on the
hearth, flung a log to the back and turned the block of
elm on the fire, so that the radiant bark glowed like burning scales. He stood, leaning against the chimney, and
looked anxiously at Gilles. He was stooped forward and
the old fine hands stretched out to the heat had gone dead
and white at the finger-tips.

[73]

"Let me pour you a drink, sir. The fast is not so strict for you. It is not as if it were Good Friday."

"You're a good lad," said Gilles gratefully. Pierre poured the wine carefully, tilting the bottle by slow degrees. He knew how to handle a wine, that youngster. But why, why was he for the cloister? Were those long legs never to grip the sides of a horse with armored knee, but sit muffled in petticoats some day on an abbot's white mule?

"I shall miss you, Pierre," he said crossly. He held out his hand for the goblet, scowling up under puckered brows.

Pierre flushed scarlet with pleasure and embarrassment. He opened his mouth, but only to stammer.

"It is nonsense," went on Gilles, ignoring him. "I do not believe that you could not get another couple of months' leave." He scowled at the young averted face and the splendid throat, rising out of the ugly cowl. "I have always felt for Charles the Fat, when he cursed the man that ever made Tutilo a monk. By the way, did you ever see the ivory he carved, the diptych at St. Gall?"

"I did not," said Pierre. O blessed Gilles, who always spoke of things, and not of sentiment. "But our Abbot told me of it. I think he would sell his soul for it. He wants it copied—you know, the vine leaves and the deer —for a capital in the cloister at Cluny."

Gilles nodded. "There has been a good deal of coveting roused by that same diptych in its time. Did you ever hear how the Abbot Salomo tricked the Bishop of Mainz out of it, and got it for St. Gall? It is a good story, but they don't like to hear it at Mainz."

Pierre sat down with a contented sigh. To sit with

[74]

Gilles was to sit with Time himself, to whom a thousand years were as yesterday. "Hearing you talk," he said suddenly and without embarrassment, "is the best thing I have got out of Paris."

Gilles looked at him with narrowed eyes. "Do not forget," he said, a little sternly, "that you heard Peter Abelard lecture on 'I said: ye are gods.'"

The young face did not redden: it went suddenly expressionless.

"I have not forgotten," he said quietly, but Gilles felt a curious hardness in the voice. Quick anger swept over him. He leaned forward, his hands gripping the arms of his chair, his huge frame half out of it, his jowl thrust into Pierre's face.

"And who," said he, "are you to condemn him?"

The movement was not calculated, but it served. The youngster shrank back, startled out of his frozen mask.

"I'm not condemning him." His voice was sharp with wretchedness. "But—but I worshiped him." He dropped his head on his hands.

Gilles sat back, his brief anger spent.

"I know," he said, "I know. It is hard to forgive one's god for becoming flesh."

Pierre de Montboissier raised his head. He was flushed with the tears he had kept back, but there was no fear of them now.

"It is not that," he said steadily. "St. Augustine himself— But it is what has happened to his mind. It is heavier, like his face now. And he does not care for any of us. He used now and then to stay and talk when the lecture was over. Hours he would talk, and we would never know we were hungry. You do not know what he

[75]

was like. His lectures, they were like a great wind that leapt suddenly, and you went with it, the trees tearing and shaking. It was like galloping horses—" He stopped breathless. "And now—"

"And now?"

"It is not fair of me to talk of him like this, but you— you know him utterly. He reads his lectures now, old lectures, and yawns reading them, and every now and then he looks at the hour-glass. None of us ever saw the, sand run down. Most of us watch for it now. And they bet if he will stay the last grains of sand. He never gives the extra lecture—you know what they call the *Extra ordinem.* Sometimes it comes back; someone asks a question, and it is like a hawk, you know when the eyelid half closes and suddenly it slides back, and he blazes down at us. But it is oftener to strike than to soar. Even then, just to see him before he stoops—" Pierre's eyes were shining in his head. They suddenly clouded.

"But they are not afraid of him now. If you heard them snickering when he comes to the lecture at six, half awake, about . . . about . . ."

Gilles nodded.

"They've made a song about it," Pierre went on savagely, like one biting on a tooth.

> "Good argument
> Hath Peter in his head,
> But better argument
> Hath Peter—"

"I can supply the rhyme," said Gilles. There was silence between them.

"God knows," the boy went on, arguing with himself,

[76]

"we are spirit and flesh. But to see the spirit becoming flesh before one's eyes. And *his* spirit."

Again Gilles nodded. "How old are you, Pierre?"

"Almost twenty-two."

"Abelard is thirty-seven. For the seven years of manhood that you have behind you, and the fifteen that are before you till you reach his age, this man never looked on a woman to lust after her." He was glowering at the young man's face, content to see it slowly redden. "He was proud enough and arrogant, but lavish—had he ever a penny? When other men gave the rind of the bacon, he gave all he had. And he would come in here to me famished, because he had forgotten to eat. He came to the age when a man's passion is fiercest, and he has begun to know how solitary his soul is, but still he was like a man walking in a dream, though I thought I saw signs of his waking. Then one day, in this room, he saw Heloise."

Pierre's head was bent, but the back of his neck, his very ears were crimson.

"God help the boy," thought Gilles, in sudden understanding. He waited a moment.

"He is not the only man," he went on quietly, "who would think her worth flinging the world away for, and heaven after it."

Pierre shivered. He did not look at Gilles. but at his twisting hands.

"They make songs," he managed to say at last, croaking, "about her too."

"And do you suppose," said Gilles with a sudden ring of triumph in his voice, "that she cares?"

Pierre looked at him, startled.

[77]

"How could she not?"

"You think," said Gilles slowly, "it is the dove and the hawk? I tell you, you have seen the mating of eagles. And yet," the ring of triumph left his voice, "I know, I know. Boy, do you think I am not myself afraid? Never have I seen such madness as this. And I wonder sometimes what the end will be."

The door opened abruptly.

"Will you see Master Alberic of Rheims," said Jehan, "for he came up the stairs after me?"

"Surely," said Gilles. He turned his face to the door. Pierre de Montboissier rose from his stool, and stood in the shadow beyond the chimney, watching a large and portly figure come through the door, and pace with dignity down the room.

"You are welcome, Alberic," said Gilles. "Man, even if I had not heard it, I would know from the very walk of you that they have made you Master of the Schools at Rheims."

"My walk?" said Alberic uncertainly, halting the procession.

"And why not? Should not the spirit be mirrored in the body? It is the sign of an ingenuous soul. How long have you been in Paris?"

"Since Palm Sunday," said Alberic. "And I must go tomorrow. But I could not take my leave without seeing our Nestor." Gilles bowed. "And I had warm greetings for you from the Archbishop."

"Raoul le Vert," said Gilles reminiscently. "But I suppose he is white enough now. Well, tell him from me, if you have not already done so, what a distinguished scholastic he has got. Bless my soul," he went on reflectively, "to think of you sitting in Gerbert's chair."

"I trust," said Alberic, "that the doctrine taught from it will be a little sounder."

"I am sure of it," said Gilles. "Safer, at any rate. No mathematics in it. The common people used to say that the devil made Gerbert a brazen head that answered all inconvenient questions for him. Much better to have it on one's own shoulders. Upon my word, Alberic, at this rate there will soon be an exodus from Paris to Rheims."

"You flatter me, Gilles," said Alberic. "Though indeed," he went on, pouting his full lips, "if the lecture I heard a day or two ago is a specimen of the fare here, it is a stony pasture enough."

A figure stepped out of the shadow. "You were unfortunate, Master Alberic" said Pierre courteously. "Whom did you hear?"

"The great Abelard himself," said Alberic. He chuckled. "A barren shallow wit. I always knew it. And would you believe it, the lecture I heard on Monday, word for word, was a lecture I heard him give three years ago at Laon, before Anselm silenced him."

Pierre de Montboissier made a step forward, but an almost imperceptible movement of Gilles's hand halted him.

"A marvelous memory yours, Alberic," said Gilles blandly. "It may be—nay, it must be—the secret of your high success. Yet it must have been a rare lecture, for you to remember it after three years."

"My memory is indeed tolerably good," said Alberic. "But I have special reason to recall this one. It was the first he had the impudence to give, and a few of us went to hear him and take note of his impertinences. It was an unheard-of thing, for a young man, unlicensed, to lecture without permission, setting himself up in opposition to that good old man."

"I am glad to hear the rights of it," said Gilles smoothly. "I had always understood that he was challenged to it."

"Challenged? Well, in a manner, yes," said Alberic. "He had had the impudence to declare that a man needs no master in theology but Holy Writ and the Fathers and his own intelligence."

"A very dangerous doctrine," said Gilles. "The half of us would find our occupation gone. To whom did he say it? Not, I hope, to old Anselm, may God rest his soul. He would have had apoplexy."

"It was not to Anselm direct," admitted Alberic. "But he had absented himself from Anselm's lectures, and some of us observed it and rebuked him for it."

"I am glad," said Gilles, "that he had so much grace. It is more than he showed to William here. Poor William; it was a good day for him when Abelard's seat was empty. But after all, William was forty-five and a fresh man: it was fine exercise for him. Abelard has a kind of respect for age. He is very civil to myself. And so you challenged the barren rascal?"

"We did."

"And he lectured, I suppose, to empty benches?"

"There are always lovers of novelty," said Alberic. "And he drew the lighter sort, till Anselm silenced him."

"That was not like that good old man," said Gilles. "I never thought he looked beyond the first benches, and there, Alberic, he would see your earnest face. But I suppose you reported it to him?"

"We thought," said Alberic uncomfortably, "myself and Lotulf of Novara—"

"I never liked Lombards," said Gilles absent-mindedly. "But I forget myself. So you chased him? And Paris got the leavings of Laon. What became of Lotulf?"

"He is with me," said Alberic. "I had the good fortune to be able to retain him as my coadjutor."

"They transplant well," said Gilles. "Like Jews. So you are still hunting in couples? Well, my friend Raoul is better off even than I thought. A pair of active hounds. And long may he be able to keep them in leash. Pierre, a cup of wine for Master Alberic. No, Alberic, I insist. It must be after Vespers, and anyhow you have travelers' grace."

Pierre moved to the dresser and came again, offering Master Alberic his cup with a faintly exaggerated courtesy.

"You are a student of Master Abelard?" said Alberic, eyeing him with distaste.

Pierre bowed. "I have that good fortune."

Alberic looked him up and down.

"You are a monk of Cluny?"

"At Vézelay. I had leave from Cluny to hear Master Abelard for the winter."

"If Cluny had been what it was," said Alberic, "I doubt if you would have had it. But it has lifted up its soul to vanity and lies. When it knew the holy Hugh—"

"It knows the greatest master in Christendom, anyhow," said Pierre. He was trembling.

"Well crowed, bantam," said Gilles. "Now, Alberic,

[81]

do not have your countenance suffused. May not this one be loyal to his master, as you to the good Anselm?"

"Loyalty where loyalty is due," said Alberic. "But to a masterless man that climbed over the wall into the sheepfold, a wencher and a—"

"Pierre!" thundered Gilles. The boy's arm had swung back for a resounding smack across the large, white face. It fell to his side, and he stood breathing hard and shivering like an over-ridden colt.

Alberic looked at him, his lips tight. "Perhaps you know," he said, "if they teach you any canon law at Cluny, that that would have meant excommunication?"

Gilles raised his hand. "That will do, Alberic. Pierre, go now, but come and see me tomorrow, before you start on your journey. I have a little present for your Abbot, an Art of Writing that came to me from Monte Cassino. It might interest you too, Alberic."

He lifted his hand in easy farewell to Pierre, as he talked. The young man made him a reverence, and without a look at Alberic, turned and walked across the room. The door latched behind him.

A whistle came from Alberic's pursed lips.

"I trust," said Gilles gravely, "you are grateful to me, Alberic. I feared for a few of those fine front teeth. Man, you would have gone down like a sack of oats."

"He would have paid with a good many stripes for it," said Alberic grimly. "And what midden was that cockerel reared on?"

"His father is the Sieur de Montboissier," said Gilles. Alberic's jaw dropped. "Doubtless it would have salved your hurt," Gilles went on blandly, "to know that you had suffered at so exalted a hand. And if I am not mistaken, you will some day be telling the story in your cups that you once threatened excommunication to the Abbot of Cluny."

"That one the Abbot of Cluny?"

"As soon, I think, as the abbacy is vacant and his years allow. But see here, Alberic, you called Peter Abelard what you meant for an ill name, though when the boy is older he will know how many of us deserve it. What did you mean?"

"If you do not know that, Gilles," said Alberic, "you are the only man in Paris that does not. Except, they tell me, the poor old sheep, her uncle. It met me in the change house at Meaux. And they were singing a bawdy song under my window last night. They tell me it was one of his own. I wonder, Gilles, that you can see the old man's innocence so grossly abused. I tried to hint something of it to him myself today."

"You are sure," said Gilles smoothly, "that you would not prefer to hint something of it to the culprit? For I am expecting him, after Vespers. If a brother be overtaken in a fault, restore such an one in the spirit of meekness. Or would you rather wait for the support of your friend Lupus of Novara?"

"Lotulf," said Alberic mechanically. He had risen, but already a swift foot was coming up the stair. The arras flew back, and Abelard was in the room, filling it with a curious vibration. With the wind that swept from the door, a flame leapt on the crumbling log, and danced on the three faces.

Gilles glanced from one to the other. "God, what a bladder of lard," he thought. "And what a firebrand."

Abelard had gazed for a moment blankly at the

[83]

stranger. Then his face lit up with impish friendliness.

"Old Alberic!" said he, and reached out a hand to the doctor's hood that hung from Alberic's shoulders. "Well done, man. Rheims has got a good mastiff. And how is the terrier?"

"You speak in riddles, Master Abelard," said Alberic.

"You know him, the little sharp-nosed friend, with pink eyes, like a ferret. He used to find the scent and you gave tongue. And mind you, Gilles, our Alberic has a good bell-mouthed bay. It is the great deep chest he has. But you're putting on flesh, Alberic. And so, they tell me, am I."

Alberic moistened his lips. "If you will excuse me, Gilles," he said formally, "I shall take my leave. I am to sup with the Bishop tonight. I may take your greetings to the Archbishop? Master Abelard, your servant."

Abelard swept his doctor's cap to the knee. The procession formed, and moved out.

"Some men are born to be bishops," said Abelard. "That one walks under his miter already. But what a hill of suet!"

Gilles was wiping his hands on the skin that lay over his knees.

"You were spared that at least," he said. "If godliness makes a man's face to shine, I wish it did not also make his hands to sweat."

Abelard did not answer. He stood leaning against the chimney, just as Pierre had stood, his foot tapping on the floor. The mischief had gone from his eyes, and left them dark and smoldering. "Lucifer," thought Gilles, "but not the Light-bringer tonight. The Prince of Darkness."

"What about a drink, Peter?" he said at last. "Or had you better eat first, if you have been fasting?"

Abelard looked up. "I have been fasting, sure enough," he said, an odd under-current of bitterness in his voice. He crossed to the dresser, splashed out a cupful, and drank it at a gulp.

"That's better," he said, and came back to the fire. He was humming under his breath, the tune that was over all Paris.

> "Set now your arms on mine,
> Take we our pleasure,
> O flower of all the world—"

"Stop that," said Gilles.

Abelard smiled at him affectionately. "What do you suppose, Gilles," said he, "was the idea of fasting? To keep down the body and bring it into subjection? Or to put an edge on every sense one has? For it seems to me that whatever the body lacks in vigor, the mind makes up for. And I begin to understand the rich temptations of the Desert Fathers. Lord, what an orgy of the mind they had!"

"See here, Peter," said Gilles, "you had better go home, eat the heaviest meal you can put into you, read for a couple of hours, and go to your bed. For you are in the devil's own mood this night."

"Perhaps I am," said Abelard. He sat down by the fire again, shuddering a little. "Perhaps I am." He sat silent, brooding upon the fire. After a long time, he began to speak.

"I saw one man tonight," he said, "that had been fasting long enough. I was coming out from Vespers. He was kneeling below the Crucifix, at the foot of the stairs

to the rood-loft; and just as I was passing him, he
crumpled up. I hauled him out to Grosse Margot's and
got a glass of wine into him before he knew, and when
he came to, he could have spat it at me. Poor soul, I had
broken a ten days' fast on him. An Irishman, one of
Malachy's men from Armagh."

Gilles sat silent. Better let him talk himself out.

"He was half delirious at first, muttering the same
words over and over to himself. I could not make out the
sense, but it was a good meter. And when I had comforted him a while, and told him that where the mind
had not consented the body still kept its integrity, as
with the holy virgins that by force lost their virginity
—you are squeamish tonight, Gilles?—he got friendly
enough. And I asked him what the meter was, and the
words. So he translated me the Irish. It was a prayer, but
he said if he had been rightly himself, he should not have
been praying it till Good Friday."

Abelard had risen and had gone across the room to
the far window, faintly luminous now with the rising
moon. He stood, looking out, his head resting against the
central mullion, his arms stretched along the cross-beams.
The long, black sleeves falling from either arm drooped
like great wings. "God have mercy," said Gilles to himself, "it's a crucified Apollyon."

He turned back to the room, still leaning against the
central bar, but his arms by his side.

"Do you not want to hear it, Gilles?"

"Well?" It was all Gilles could do not to shout at him.

The arms went out again, the face bent forward, the
eyes gleaming out of the white devil's mask of the face.

"May some fruit from the Tree of Thy Passion
Fall on us this night."

Gilles crossed himself. After a while he spoke.

"Go home, Abelard," he said, as if he spoke to a child. "You are not yourself. And for God's sake, eat your supper and go to bed."

"I'll go to bed," said Abelard lightly. "I promise you that. I'll go to bed. There, Gilles," the mockery had slipped from his voice, "don't fret. Man, you'd think I had been saying a Black Mass instead of a poor Irishman's litany. I'll eat my supper, and read a while, and go to bed. Shall I send Jehan up to you?"

"He will be here with my supper shortly," said Gilles. "Will you stay and have it with me, Peter?"

Abelard shook his head. The faint smoldering came back to his eyes.

"I have fasted long enough," he said. "I'll be getting home. Good-night, Gilles. Sleep." He was gone.

Gilles sat sunk in his chair. "*They say that Paradise and Calvary, Christ's cross and Adam's tree, stood in one place,*" he muttered to himself. Slowly he got out of his chair, and crossed to where his stool was set below the crucifix, lowering himself painfully upon his gouty knees.

O Lamb of God that takest away the sin of the world: have mercy upon us.

O Lamb of God that takest away the sin of the world: have mercy upon us.

O Lamb of God that takest away the sin of the world: receive our prayer.

Jehan, coming in with his dish of trout, stood gazing at a sight he had not seen for fifteen years.

The moon, two days past its Easter fullness, shone into the window of Heloise's room, and across the bed, but her face was in shadow, and she was fast asleep. Abelard stood at the foot of the bed, looking down at her. A moment, a touch of the hand he could put out would wake her; but until then, what leagues she was away! He would not wake her: kneel by her for a while and lay down his head on the bed and feel the dear warmth of her so close. It might exorcise the devil that had seemed to enter into him with the Irishman's litany:

> May some fruit from the Tree of Thy Passion
> Fall on us this night.

Yet the words were holy enough, holy with a mystery beyond even the *Pange lingua gloriosi*. Was it that for a soul like his even holiness was turned to poison? With a half-convulsive shiver he gripped her close.

She wakened: it was always her way to waken so, not sleepily, rubbing her eyes, but wide awake, with the clear depths gazing straight up at him. She was silent for a while, gazing so, and smiling. Then memory came into them.

"Dear, what is it? Are you ill?"

He shook his head.

"I could not sleep. I thought if I saw you, sat by you for a while, I might go back to bed and sleep. I did not mean to wake you. Let me hold you, Heloise."

She sat up and put her arms about him. He laid his head on her shoulder, with a sigh of content.

"Is that better?"

"That's better. Oh, Heloise, hold me close."

[88]

She held him closer; he was shivering, every moment more violently.

"Peter, you are ill. You have taken a chill with fasting, and it's fever. Let me get up and get you a hot drink."

"I am not ill. Oh, my love, my love. Let me have you, Heloise. If I do not have you tonight, something will take me from you. There is something abroad tonight. I felt it at Vespers in Notre Dame, and when the Irishman was raving. I shall lose you tonight if I do not have you and hold you against all the devils in hell—"

"Peter, hush! Dear love, it is Holy Week."

"Holy Week! O God, don't I know it, don't I know it's Holy Week?—

> May some fruit from the Tree of Thy Passion
> Fall—"

"Peter, hush!" She was kissing him to stop the wild torrent of blasphemous speech, and trembling too. Something of his madness was quivering in her blood. Now his kisses were raining upon her like a fiery hail. Hell fire it might be, but never had she known such burning ecstasy. She sank back, her arms outstretched to him.

Slowly the bar of moonlight crept across the floor. They lay cheek to check in a quiet trance: the moon itself was not more still. Heloise sighed, a little happy sigh: her eyclashes fluttered against his cheek, and he laughed softly and drew the coverlet closer round her. A cloud passed over the moon, and the room was full of a warm darkness. Outside a stair creaked. He started.

"What's that?"

"Guibert," she whispered. "He is always late to bed."

"Are you sure?"

"I hear him every night that I am awake."

The steps were mounting slowly, uncertain, dragging steps.

"He must be drunk tonight," whispered Heloise. "Mostly he is lighter on his feet."

There was a moment's pause on the landing.

"He passes my door, and Grizzel's, and goes up the ladder to the loft. Listen."

The uncertain footsteps came on and stopped. Someone was fumbling with the latch of the door. It opened. Abelard started up. It was Fulbert who came through it, shading the candle with his hand. He closed the door behind him and stood a moment blinking, till the candle flame steadied itself and shone clear on their faces. He stood there looking at them, and they at him. Then he lifted his hands with a cry no louder than a bat's shriek, swayed, and slid to the ground. The candlestick falling made more noise than he. The candle rolled from it on the floor, and lay there, still burning.

In a moment Abelard was beside him, slipping his arm beneath his shoulder. He was breathing hoarsely, stertorously, and his mouth was awry.

"Hold the light, Heloise," said Abelard. "It's a stroke."

There was no answer. He reached for the candle with his left hand, set it up, and turned to look at her.

She was sitting on the edge of the bed, her dark hair flowing over her shoulders and her rounded knees, looking straight at him, but seeing neither him nor the wreckage in his arms. Her eyes were like the windows of a roofless house.

"Heloise!" he cried, his voice sharp with fear.

[90]

She shook her head. "It is over," she said, under her breath. Then coming to herself with a shudder, she looked at him, but this time with recognition.

"Here!" she cried, and springing from the bed, she flung back the covers. "Lay him down here. I'll waken Grizzel."

CHAPTER VII

I TELL you, Bernard, the thing is impossible."

Bernard of Clairvaux looked tranquilly down at Gilles. "With God all things are possible."

"Amen," said Gilles. "But by your leave, Bernard, you and He are not yet identical."

The eyes, deep set in the ravaged face, lit up with a smile of extraordinary charm.

"Thank God," said Gilles, "you can still laugh. Even at yourself. And if you smile like that at young Robert, he will eat out of your hand all the way back to Clairvaux. But I doubt if you will keep him, once you have him."

"I shall keep him," said Bernard. His lips set.

"And your warrant?"

"*Those that Thou gavest me I have kept, and not one of them is lost, save the son of perdition.* And, please God, Robert shall not be that."

"I do not imagine," said Gilles soberly, "that it pleased Him to lose Judas. But He lost him. Has it never struck you, Bernard, that God has more respect for the free will of the creature He made in His own image than you have?"

"It was free will that damned us," said Bernard.

[91]

"That," said Gilles, "is not the point."

Bernard moved impatiently. "I have no logic, Gilles," he began, "and beside you I am an ignorant man. All I know is that if a man has once seen the face of God, as young Robert did, and then turns from it, it were better for him that he had never been born; for he has crucified the Son of God afresh, and put Him to an open shame. And I have vowed not to break my fast till I have seen him face to face, and pleaded with him, on my knees, to come back. And his penance I shall share with him myself." He was looking straight before him, forgetting to whom he spoke, and the voice that had been harsh and constrained as he began had dropped to a deeper and strangely moving note.

Gilles looked at the young clenched hands, knotted with rheumatism—rheumatism at twenty-six—the thin stooped figure. Did not someone tell him that the Abbot's cell at Clairvaux was so built that he could not stand upright, nor stretch himself out upon his bed?

"If you speak to him like that," he said gently, "I think he will come back. But, Bernard," his eyes had gone to the window beyond which the white pigeons flashed and tumbled in the blue air of May, "forgive me: are you so sure that to leave Clairvaux, where no man speaks unless in a whisper and the damp drips down the refectory walls and the brethren kneel in green slime on the chapel floor, and to go back to the kind house of Cluny, where he was reared and where his bed if it was hard was dry, is to turn from the face of God, and crucify His Son afresh?"

"I do. If a man puts his hand to the plow and looks back—"

"Bernard," Gilles's voice was suddenly stern, "he has

turned not from God's face, but from your face. He has not crucified the Son of God afresh, but he is the first deserter from your abbey that was to be the City of God upon earth; and the thing that he has crucified is your pride."

The Abbot flinched, but there was no anger in the deep eyes, only perplexity.

"My pride? Gilles, is it possible that any man on this earth should think me proud?"

"Proud? I tell you, Bernard, there is only one man in Europe prouder than the Abbot of Clairvaux, and that is Peter Abelard."

A spasm of anger contorted the Abbot's face, but only for a moment. It was followed by a look of genuine wretchedness.

"And now," said Gilles remorsefully, "you will be using the discipline on those thin shoulders for weeks, for fear I may be right."

"God knows you may be," said Bernard. "And that I should have given you cause to think it is wretchedness enough."

"Forget it," said Gilles. "And what is one solitary son of Belial like myself against the united voice of Christendom?"

The arras parted and Heloise stood, the eager expectancy on her face slowly ebbing as she saw an unfamiliar presence.

"Forgive me, Gilles," she said. "I did not know that you had a stranger with you."

"Come in, child," said Gilles. "This is the Abbot of Clairvaux."

She knelt dutifully to kiss the Abbot's ring, then rose,

[93]

regarding him. The two stood face to face for a moment, searching one another's eyes, and Gilles noted a curious resemblance. Not of feature, but of spirit. They both, he could see, lived and moved in some other life than their own: both had the same inner radiance, the same clear line of cheekbone and jaw. The soft roundness was gone from Heloise's chin: she was thinner and there were dark shadows beneath her eyes. Yet never, thought Gilles, had she looked so starry.

"My daughter," said the Abbot suddenly, "I think some day I shall call you sister."

Heloise's head drew back as a fawn's might from the hand of a stranger. Her eyes were startled.

"What do you mean, my Father?"

"The life of the spirit is more to you already than the life of the flesh. And how shall you not some day be in subjection to the Father of Spirits, and live? Have you never thought of taking the vows?"

She caught her breath. "Never."

"I had a brother," Bernard went on, inexorably. "He had your look. He was married to a young wife and had two fair sons. He struggled long, but in the end he gave them up, and has come to live with his brethren in our bare house at Clairvaux. For there is no half-way house with such as you. Let you once give, you give, I think, for eternity."

"And what, Father," said Heloise quickly, "if one has already given? If there is no more oil in the lamp?" Her smile was faintly mocking. She turned from him decisively. "But I must not stay. My uncle is watching for me. I only came," she added, "to bring you this letter, Gilles."

[94]

Gilles took it from her, without glancing at the super-scription. "There is no answer?" he asked. "I need not read it now?"

"There is no answer," said Heloise. She was watching him anxiously. He put it between the leaves of the Horace in his lap, and closed the book upon it, with a little reassuring nod. She bent to touch his hand, knelt before the Abbot, and was gone.

Bernard crossed over to the hearth.

"Who is she, Gilles? I have never seen a face that had so markedly the makings of a saint. She looked to me as Our Lady might, when she sang *Magnificat*."

"She is niece to one of our canons," said Gilles briefly. "Her name is Heloise."

Bernard stood rigid. "Not Abelard's whore?"

"She would, I think, choose so to describe herself."

Bernard opened his mouth to speak, and shut it again.

"That's right, Bernard," said Gilles drily. "Think better of it."

"That one can go about, transparent seeming to the crystalline soul within, and that soul be mired with the filthiest sin of the flesh! Truly, God's ways are past finding out."

"I am glad you think so, Bernard," said Gilles tranquilly. "You thought you had the key to them a little while ago."

Again the look of anger, again the frank recognition. Curse him, thought Gilles, the man is a saint.

"I do not believe it is His purpose it should always be so," said Bernard slowly. "I shall keep vigils for her."

"As Paphnutius did for Thais?"

Bernard had come across the room and was looking

[95]

inscrutably down at the massive fleshly countenance upturned to his.

"Why do you come to see me, Bernard?" said Gilles
irritably. "A heathen man and a publican. To do me
good?"

"No," said Bernard. He thought for a while. "I am
afraid," he said simply, "it is only because I like you,
Gilles."

Gilles flung out his hands and groaned. "What is one
to do with a man like that? But, Bernard," he looked up,
his eyes bright with mischief, "it has given me a thought,
to edification. Two kinds of people you love: lost souls
like me, black sheep, goats even. And your own fold,
that blessed little shivering ague-stricken flock of yours
at Clairvaux. But the brethren, the plain gray sheep of the
other folds—you have small love or charity for them."

Bernard stood, frowning thoughtfully.

"God forgive me if you are right, Gilles. And my
anger rises so that I fear you are. I shall put my mind to
it. But I must be going."

"Well, be gentle with young Robert."

The Abbot nodded. He lifted his hands: "The grace
of Our Lord Jesus Christ, the love of God, and the communion and fellowship of the Holy Ghost be with you."

"Amen," said Gilles. "The uncanny thing about you,
Bernard, is that you invoke the communion and fellowship of the Holy Ghost upon me as if you meant it. It
leaves me uncomfortable for half an hour."

The Abbot flung back his head in a delighted shout
of laughter. "He would not find you such ill company
as you think, Gilles," said he, and went downstairs.

"That," said Gilles, to himself, "was very handsome

[96]

of him " He sighed, and opened his Horace. The letter
lay there, addressed in Heloise's hand to Master Gilles de
Vannes, but there was a mark after the "Vannes." He
held it thoughtfully. God help them, he thought, they
had not seen each other for a fortnight. Abelard should
be here any moment now. A pity the child could not
have stayed: but she had said her uncle was watching.
Truly, as Bernard said, God's ways are past finding out.
Why, when the old man had his stroke, could he not
have died instead of living to make the house a hell?
Living, too, with a strange new energy of hate. And
that old bearded witch of a Grizzel not much better. It
was an ill house for that young creature. But her courage!
The love of these two had always been beyond his comprehending: it was beyond it still. Separation and agony
seemed to have purged whatever dross was in it: it burned
with a clearer flame. Abelard, back in his old quarters in
the Maison du Poirier, and half-starved again with Guibert's poor providing and worse cooking, was like the
Abelard of that first September. He had begun to write
again in the long evenings, till it was dark enough for
him to pace up and down beneath the house, if he might
catch a glimpse of her at the window. But only twice had
he dared to find his way in. Old Grizzel was on the
watch, long after Fulbert had gone to bed, and it was
only when she went out to her crony in the Rue Cocatrice that it was possible. But he had no complaint. He
never spoke to Gilles of his own misery, only of hers.
That, Gilles could see, was his perpetual torment. And
yet it seemed to him, watching and pondering, that they
knew ecstasy now as they had never known it, when love
was easy and warm on the hearthstone.

[97]

There was the familiar foot, hurrying up the stair. The door burst open, and once again Gilles saw eagerness suddenly wiped from a face. This face had strangely got its youth again.

"She was here, Peter," he said, "but the old man was watching for her. She left you a letter."

Abelard caught at it and went over to the far window, turning his back on Gilles to read it. Gilles heard the sound of the breaking seal, and then a sudden exclamation. There fell a long silence.

Abelard turned and came slowly down the room. His eyes looked dazed. He swallowed once or twice before he spoke.

"She says," he began at last, his voice so low that Gilles could hardly hear it, "she says she is going to have a child."

Gilles looked at him in silence. The magnitude of the calamity had taken his speech from him.

At last he spoke. "It may not be so, Peter. She may easily be mistaken."

Abelard shook his head. "She says that she is sure. She says," his mouth began to tremble, "that she has been reading Aristotle to find out." He broke down, helplessly. "Reading Aristotle, that little lonely child. Not a woman to speak to but that damned hag. Reading Aristotle, my little one, my little one. And I brought her to this."

Gilles pulled himself together. "See here, Peter. Even if it is true, she is happy. She was here today. I tell you I never saw her so—so blessed. Bernard of Clairvaux saw her. He said she looked like Mary when she sang *Magnificat*."

"I know." Abelard raised his head, rubbing his eyes

[98]

viciously. "Her letter is like that. It *is* a *Magnificat*. She is wildly happy. She says she thought for a long time it was too good to be true."

The two looked at each other in bewilderment. "It is the way of women sometimes," said Gilles, "when—when they love the father of it."

Abelard flushed scarlet. "But, Gilles, what is she to do? The old man is cruel enough with her now, when there is no open scandal. You see, his having a stroke like that made it natural for me to move out of the house. He is like a child that shuts his eyes and thinks nobody can see him. But this—there will be no dissembling this. Even as it is—I cannot tell you, Gilles, the very thought of it drives me mad. Heloise pretended she had hurt herself. But I saw one bruise. It is as if hate gave him strength. And I think he hates her now. When I think of her alone in that house with him and that hell-cat Grizzel—"

"I have thought sometimes," said Gilles, "that the old tenderness had come back."

Abelard shook his head. "Only, I think, to torture him. And always he remembers how he was deceived. Do you know, Gilles, I could find it in my heart to pity him? Even that night, the poor soul had no suspicion when he came upstairs. He was creeping up to waken Heloise, because he felt sick. And he trusted me."

"Don't think of it now," said Gilles.

Abelard got to his feet. "She must not stay in that house," he said slowly. "That is one thing certain. But—Gilles, I have it; I shall take her to Brittany, to Denise."

"Denise?"

"I told you, the sister who married Hugh the Stranger. They are living there still—at Le Palais. Denise has half a dozen already, and I told you, she has the kindness of the earth. And she always was fond of me." He was walking up and down, his eyes bright. "This is the end of May. Heloise says two months. That means Christmas. We have only to wait till the end of June, and I can ride with her." He was transfigured, as eager as a small boy planning a holiday. "Gilles, I must see her. To ride together, all the way to Brittany—and we shall have the whole summer, I need not come back till St. Rémy, October 1st. It was my own choice to begin in September. And later on I'll have a proxy here and go back to her, for Christmas." He turned and stood looking out of the window, suddenly silent.

"Well, it is as it should be," said Gilles gravely. "Where should your son be born, but in his father's house?"

BOOK II
BRITTANY

April–May 1118

CHAPTER I

"T<i>his then, as I have already said, is the definition of
sin: sin is the will to hold or to follow after that
which righteousness forbids, and from which a
man is free to abstain.</i>" The April sun came out from behind a racing cloud and turned the parchment molten,
but Abelard, too absorbed in Augustine's argument to be
aware of his own discomfort, wrote on, his eyes screwed
up and his left hand cupping a bay of shadow on the page.
"<i>I say then that there is no sin where there is no personal
will to sin: but I would have it understood that I speak
of sin, not of the punishment of sin: of that punishment
I have elsewhere said what is to be said.</i>" Abelard was
smiling as he wrote, recognizing with a twist of irony
an arrogance so like his own. The quotation finished, he
sat back, aware at last that his eyes were smarting; he
looked from the almost invisible script on the dazzling
page to the window, and saw a single branch of pear
blossom from the ancient tree that grew against the western gable, intolerably white against the blackness of the
bark. For a little while he sat, his hands outspread in the
bar of light that fell across the table, remembering the
Irish gloss he had seen in a MS. at Laon that Dubthach
had shown him: "Good it is to see the April sunlight
flickering on this page." But to work in this blaze was
impossible: he rose and began to drag the massive table
across the room to its summer halting place by the north

window. Odd, he reflected, that one can only think, to
call it thinking, in the gray light of the north in which
no living thing thrives, except man's mind only. He stood
for a moment looking out at the Parvis Notre Dame and
an ancient beggar sunning himself on the steps of the
cathedral. It would soon be time for Compline. He sat
down, and again began to write.

"Chapter CXLVI. *Quod idem peccatum non puniat
Deus hic et in futuro:* that God doth not punish the same
sin here and hereafter." The Q, he thought, was always a
good initial for illumination: he laid down his pen and
took a pencil to draw the great ellipse, lest he should
forget and leave no place for Simon's gold-leaf: then to
please himself added the tail-piece like the tongue of a
belt that turned the O into a Q, and as he drew, the tail-
piece became the branch of a pear tree with flowers on
it, and suddenly there sat on it a long-tailed bird. The
branch had curved along the line of script, and the bird
thrust a jaunty tail between the *hic* and the *futuro,* this
world and the next. That curve, thought Abelard, suddenly aware of what he drew, ought to be the tongue of
a dragon with little flames leaping upon it, instead of
pear tree blossom and an impudent fowl, making light
of the judgments of God. But perhaps it was the truth
of his own mood that came out in what his hand unwit-
tingly drew, and he began to ponder on the law of the
human heart, that two years ago, when he made these
notes which he was now copying, he had been more inti-
mately concerned as to the nature and judgment of sin
than now when for eighteen months he had been living
in it, and that sin, moreover, the sin of fornication. He
thrust the word at himself deliberately, but his mind took

it indifferently: it fell away from him like a hail-stone from armor. Fornication was the goblin mask they put on the sweetest sin of the seven. And his sin was not fornication. It was Heloise.

He took up his pen again and turned to his rough draft. His notes had only the reference this time, and he reached for his Origen and began turning the pages. "The twenty-fourth chapter of Leviticus and the fifteenth verse. *If a man curse his God, he shall bear his iniquity. But if he name the name of God, he shall die the death.* What? Shall he who has cursed God escape the penalty of death, while he who has but named Him dies? Surely it is a graver fault to curse God than to name Him, even though to name Him in jest? Rather should he that has cursed the name of God be punished straightway: enough for him who names His name in wantonness and vanity to bear his sin. Now, that it is a graver sin to curse God than to name Him, we cannot doubt. It remains for us to show that it is a far graver thing to bear one's sin, to have it about with one, than to pay the fine of death. For this death which is the penalty of sin, is the payment of that sin for which it is ordered to be inflicted. The sin is absolved by the pain of death, nor is there aught left for the finding of the Day of Judgment and the pain of the everlasting fire. But he who receives his sin, who has it about with him and companies with it and is purged by no penalty or pain: it passes over with him after death, and he who paid no debt in time shall pay the torments of eternity. You see, therefore, how much graver it is to bear a sin than to atone by death: for this death is given as an expiation, or manumission; and before the Lord, the righteous Judge, shall no man, saith the prophet, be

judged twice. Where there is no expiation, the sin re-
maineth, to be dealt with in the everlasting fires. I can
summon you witnesses from the divine books, Reuben
and Judah, speaking to their father Jacob, when they
would have Benjamin with them to Egypt. For Reuben
said to his father, 'Slay my two sons if I bring not Benjamin back to thee.' But Judah said, 'If I bring him not unto
thee, then let me bear the blame for ever.' And Jacob,
knowing that what Judah had promised was a far graver
thing, did not entrust his son to Reuben, who had chosen
the lighter penalty, but handed him to Judah, knowing
how grave was his choice. Men are wont to complain
against God and say: Why do the unrighteous suffer no
ill in this life, and all distresses fall upon the lovers of
God? They know not that the judgments of God are an
abyss."

It was a strange and subtle and colorless world, thought
Abelard, sprinkling sand upon his page, this world that
Origen lived in: to read him after Augustine was like
passing over from that warm bar of light into the gray
north light of intellectual vision, and though Origen had
his own high eloquence, it was a vibration like the vibration of stars on a night of frost. *"And some have made
themselves eunuchs for the kingdom of heaven's sake."*
What high exaltation had driven him to it, or what torment of the hungry senses?

"Procul a mea— Far from my house be thy frenzy, O
goddess!"

Gilles de Vannes had quoted it, when he first spoke of
Origen, and had read him the *Attis;* but then had put
Catullus from him, saying it was almost a blasphemy to

speak of the mad priest of Cybele in the same breath with Origen, the noblest of all the Fathers; and that beside him Augustine ranted like a declaiming schoolboy, and Jerome droned like a cloister beehive.

And yet, argued Abelard, intellectual eminence aside, had not Augustine chosen the better way, like St. Paul, to fight his body rather than disarm it? And was it not the heat and passion of the whole man, rather than the effortless austerity of the sterile man, that gave his prose its kindling power of fire? To which Gilles had gravely answered that it was natural for the northern races to prefer heat to light; and had then turned upon himself and declared that Abelard was right, that so long as men were in the body they must have the sacraments of bread and wine, and the Logos must become flesh: and then in that husky, disturbing voice of his had begun quoting the passage from the Tenth Book of the *Confessions*. "*Late, late have I loved Thee, O Beauty most old and yet most new. . . . Thou didst call and very loud and didst break through my deafness. Thou didst shine and my darkness was scattered. Thou didst touch me, and I burned for thy peace.*"

Abelard rose, and was restlessly ordering the litter of books and parchments on the table. He could not escape it. That word peace was the most dangerous to his tranquil indifference, his living satisfaction, the heaven of body and spirit that he had found in Heloise. He had described it to her once, recklessly adapting St. Peter Damian's *Paradise*.

> "What they have they still desire, eager and yet satisfied."
> —Avidi et semper pleni, quod habent desiderant.

He had sung it to her one night before they slept, riding down to Brittany last June. They had halted for the night in open country on the Landes de Vion—he had of set purpose avoided the guesthouse of the abbey at Solesmes—and she had fallen asleep with little movements of her head against him, huddled in the hollow under his arm. But he had lain awake. The thing that he had rashly invoked was stronger than he: he could no more halt the inexorable procession of those tremendous verses than he could halt a procession carrying the Host. And lying there, the ancient marching rhythm of the legions tramping in his brain, he saw them go by, the goodly fellowship whose beginning no man knows, whose ranks no man can number.

> "O Christ, when I at last my arms lay down,
> Bring me, Thy soldier, to Thy blessed town,
> O Thou that art the soldiers' palm and crown.
>
> The battle knows no end; give me Thy power.
> Deny me not Thy peace, when comes my hour.
> Deny me not Thyself, the eternal dower."

It was long before he slept, and when he wakened with the coldness of rain upon his face, it was barely dawn. He had risen gently, so as not to wake Heloise, arranged his cloak so that the hood covered her face, and moved out of the copse of trees. Guibert lay beside the horses, a thin shank protruding under his cloak: pitiful, thought Abelard, the squalor of the human body asleep. But the whole world was squalid, under this ominous light. The river below was a dead snake, the hills and the clouds alike huddled and shapeless and deformed, misshapen abortions. He stood for a while, oppressed and sunken within himself. So, he thought, the world must have looked to Adam, when he first wakened outside Paradise. *Squalet et ipse dies—*

> "Daylight grew squalid: underneath his feet
> He saw a narrower earth; above his head
> Hung a remoter heaven, with moaning stars."

He had been looking east towards Malicorne, where the sky seemed heaviest; but the wind was blowing from the west, and he turned to gauge what promise there might be for the day. Even as he turned, the clouds broke, only a hand's breadth: and he looked straight into blue heaven. Something stung in his eyes to see it there, so radiant, so tender, so unaware. "Peace in Thy heaven" —the words rang in his head, coming from he knew not where. He stood dumb, a slow fear mounting in him like the uprising of a cold spring. It was as though he had seen his destiny: *and having Thee, to have naught else beside.* He was shaking now; he caught himself praying, broken snatches of prayer, that God would save him from Himself: and when a great black low-drifting cloud swept up from beyond the Sarthe and covered his eternity, he sighed with relief. A soft muzzle thrust itself over his shoulder: he felt the warm breath through those velvet nostrils on his cheek. "O brother horse, most excellent of God's creatures!" He looked about, to tether her where the grass was sweeter than the edge of the burnt heath, and Guibert woke, and they made a fire as they used to do when they were small boys fishing in the Sanguèze. Guibert had caught trout last night, with his hands, he said, under a great stone, and he speared them on sticks and grilled them above the hot wood

ashes, a deal more handily than ever he managed grid
or saucepan in Paris. And by the time Heloise had
wakened, the sun was shining, and the shadows of the
clouds moving over the fields as quiet as sheep, and the
terror and vision of the morning seemed only a bad
dream.

More than ever, in the days that came after. Sometimes in the night Abelard remembered his vision, and
knew that experience had already proved it a lie. For he
knew peace. Each day the quiet flood of it rose and filled
the hours, from his first waking with the slow creak of
the well-rope in the court, to the evenings when he
would go down at sunset to meet Heloise bringing up the
ducks from the river. Sometimes they would have gone
far afield, but at sight of her they would come, marshal-
ing themselves in a little fleet, moving stilly through
the quiet reflections on the water, their soft intermittent
gabble so remote from their morning quackings and scut-
terings, and one by one would land and lurch a little
and shake their tails and paddle up the cart track to the
dark, ill-smelling little house in which they spent their
nights. Sometimes a young one would walk affectedly
past the open door and look hopefully about the yard,
but would suddenly lose courage and scuttle undignified
for home. Heloise would wait till the last adventurous
straggler had gone in, and then slide the wooden bolt.
She had explained to Abelard that they had to be brought
in at night, or they would lay their eggs out in the marsh-
land where they might never be found, or be hatched
out into wild things again; and Abelard listened gravely
and asked questions that she might tell him what he had
known since he was five. He was never weary of watch-

ing her. Convent and city-bred, for the first time she had come to her own place, and her own people. It was a little fief. Hugh the Stranger went out with his men in the hay harvest, and Denise was her own dairy-woman. She would not let Heloise help her there, the pans were too heavy, but the girl had a lucky hand with living things, and soon the chickens ran to meet her as shrilly as they did to Denise. Agnes and Agatha, two of the bright-headed creatures that Abelard remembered tumbling like puppies in the orchard, now leggy little girls, followed her about like the shadows of fawns. And in the long September twilights, before he left for Paris, she would sit and help Hugh the Stranger with his tallies, as she used to help Godric at Argenteuil: the two baskets of crab apples that Helvis paid for her cottage, the cartload of turf that Hucbald owed for his cutting in the bogland where the Sanguèze rose, the four perches of autumn plowing that Nicholas was to be forgiven, because of the lameness of his mare. He had left Paris to come back to her on the Vigil of St. Thomas the Apostle: when he reached her on Christmas Eve, his son was already three days old.

They christened him Peter Astrolabe on Epiphany. Hugh the Stranger privately thought it an outlandish name; but he had ridden into Nantes and sold his silver chain with wolf's-head clasps, to buy him a silver cup. He had never forgotten how Abelard stood by him when Berengar found Denise was with child to a landless man. It was Heloise who chose the name: Abelard knew it was because of the nights that she lay solitary in his high turret room and watched through the arrow slits the quiet movement of the stars. Abelard reached again for

the calendar he had made, and counted, as he had already
counted a hundred times, the days remaining before he
gave his last lecture on the Vigil of St. Peter and St. Paul.
He would leave Paris that very night, the 28th of June.
Indeed, what with the number of Saints' days between,
he might as well make it June 23rd, the Vigil of St. John
the Baptist. Hard riding would do it; and so, ten days
before she would be looking for him, he would be waiting on horseback at the ford, as the first stars came out,
and see her coming down the cart track in the dusk.

"For this, for this the envious gods deny us immortality."

But meantime—he straightened his shoulders with a
quick sigh, and reached for his notes. Jerome on Nahum
the Prophet. Chapter I. Verse 9. *"There shall arise no
second tribulation: thus saith the Lord, I have stricken
once, and I shall not strike again."* Once again there was
no extract, but the reference only. Abelard turned over
the pile of books on the table: Origen on the Epistle to
the Romans, Boethius *De Trinitate*, Ambrose *De Sacra-
mentis*, Isidore *De summo bono*, Chrysostom on the
Epistle to the Hebrews; Jerome *Ad Rufinum*, Jerome on
the Epistle to the Corinthians. But Jerome on the Prophets was gone. He sat scowling, wondering if Guibert
had had the effrontery to sell it, like the Hilarius *De
Trinitate* that he had found being copied at Simon's a
month ago. Hardly. He had had enough of the fear of
God put in him to keep him from that, surely. Then his
eye lightened: he had left it with Heloise in Brittany. Yet
his memory still teased him: he could swear that he had
copied out the passage somewhere. There was something
about Sodom and Gomorrah. Something too about Ezek-

iel. That was it. He must have copied it for his unfinished commentary on Ezekiel, two years ago.

The manuscript, not yet bound, was in a cedarwood chest at the other end of the room. Abelard leant the lid back against the wall, and burrowed among the furs and parchments for a while, smelling its dark fragrance, then, straightening himself, stood beside it, turning over the pages, his mouth sardonic over the callow sententiousness of the man who had written them. As ignorant of life, he thought, as a half-feathered jackdaw. *"And one put up a wall, and lo, another daubed it with untempered mortar."* Untempered mortar, indeed. *"And lo the wall is no more, neither they that daubed it."*

"What is the vine more than any other tree? Will men take a pin of it to hang any vessel thereon?" He smiled as he remembered Gilles's ribald comment on that—could the man find nothing better to do with a vine than hang mugs on it? *Thus saith the Lord concerning the Ammonites . . . Aholah and Aholibah. . . . Thou sealest up the sum, full of wisdom and perfect in beauty.* He turned over the pages impatiently, uncertain where to find the paragraph he sought. And though in a little while he stood quiet, looking down at one page, it was not the passage that he was seeking. It was a long time before he came to look for it again.

"And the word of the Lord came unto me, saying, Son of Man, behold I shall take away the desire of thine eyes at a stroke, and thou shalt not mourn nor weep. . . . And in the morning I spoke unto the people, and in the evening my wife died."

The bell of Notre Dame had begun ringing for Compline, but he did not hear it; and when it ceased, and

the air no longer hummed with its great bourdon, he was
still unaware. The *Nunc Dimittis* and the *Te lucis ante
terminum* were sung: the prayer for a quiet night and a
perfect end breathed through the cathedral: God's mercy
was sought for those that waked, His peace for those that
slept: Paris was commended for another night to the
keeping of God almighty and merciful, Father, Son, and
Holy Ghost; and still he had not stirred. When he did
come to himself he was recalled by no outward sound or
sight: it was as though the tide on which he had been
carried out to a spiritual desolation beyond anything he
had ever dreamed, turned of its own volition, and brought
him back to a familiar shore. He stooped to put the
manuscript back into the chest and closed the lid, very
carefully; then, with the same dazed gentle movements,
he came slowly down the room to the west window.
Dimly he knew that he must have light. He pulled a stool
over to it and sat down close by it, his hands spread out
on the warm sill, breathing slow breaths, as a man might
who knows the knife still in his side, and dares not move
lest he feel again the searing agony. The fear that had
maddened him that night in Holy Week was certainty
now. Somehow, some day, they would take her from
him. And he would live, live years, live his long life, without her.

A sparrow came on the window-sill and turned his
head from side to side, looked hard at a piece of mortar,
pecked at it, and flew away with a brisk whirring of
wings. Someone was frying fish in oil: the warm smell
of it came up to him through the cool remoteness of the
pear tree blossom, and he blessed it. People were standing
about their doors in the Rue du Sablon: Pigeon the cart-

wright had a yard where one could hire hand-carts, and
an old man was trundling one back over the cobblestones,
and shouting cheerful greetings as he came. Abelard
looked down into the little street: for the first time he
noticed how bowed most of the shoulders were, how
lined the women's faces. Did life break every man, he
wondered: and was there no one over thirty-five who
had not some secret agony, some white-faced fear? Half
one's life one walked carelessly, certain that some day
one would have one's heart's desire: and for the rest of it,
one either goes empty, or walks carrying a full cup, afraid
of every step. *None but he who has seen the light
knoweth what that night is.* The poor roofs on which he
looked were suddenly transparent to him, transparent as
the wrinkled faces: and he saw nothing anywhere but
hunger for love or for bread.

A small figure turned the corner from the river, and
came slowly down the street, making for the Parvis. It
was a shabby figure, like a molting sparrow, and as if
aware of its own shabbiness, it walked with bent head,
its shoulders hunched, and looking for no salutation. The
men on their doorsteps looked curiously after it as it
went by. Abelard watched, deliberately allowing every
detail of its ignominy to sink into his heart. This was his
doing: *the work of our hands establish Thou it.* Deliberately he called to mind the exquisite china skin, the silken
silver hair, the neat bantam strut that so delighted Gilles,
the small important gossip about the Chapter, the wide
baby's smile when he spoke of Heloise. That was Fulbert
once, who now slunk along the street, his unkempt locks
straggling below a greasy skullcap, the stains of food on
his cassock. Abelard had never yet seen him face to face,

for Fulbert avoided every encounter, would turn into a strange house rather than meet him on the street. And Gilles was oddly reluctant to speak of him. Once when Abelard, conscience-struck, had begun to ask if nothing could be done to look after him, Gilles shook his head. "You had better face it," he said briefly, "the man is mad. Look to yourself, for he would do you a mischief if he could. But that apart, you will be happier if you do not let your mind run upon him."

With that, Abelard had been content. But tonight, in this new sensitiveness, he had gone deeper. Mad, yes: but did one ever think of the agony that came before madness? In what deep waters had that small cheerful brain struggled till it drowned, and in what dark places had it wandered, till it for ever lost its way? Even at the height of his passion, Abelard had winced when that trusting hand was laid upon his sleeve. He knew that Paris mocked at the old man's credulity, deriding it for complacent vanity. But there was more than that, thought Abelard. One does not easily suspect where one loves, and Fulbert had loved not Heloise only, but himself. It was the supreme betrayal.

The forlorn figure was crossing the Parvis now, immeasurably tiny in its emptiness. He was not making for the main cloister gate: another moment, and he would turn into the ruelle to the Rue Sainte Marine, and so down the Rue de l'Enfer to the dark house above the river from which the light had been stamped out. It was with no knowledge of what he would do or say that Abelard leapt to his feet, flung his hood over his shoulder, and dashed down the stair. Only he knew that somehow he must see Fulbert face to face, and hold him till he could tell him that at least he knew the full measure of his wrong. Most folk were indoors at their supper, and there was no one to stay him, yet the old man, once in sight of his refuge, must have hurried at the last, for with all Abelard's striding he only overtook him on the step of his own house. He had hurried even more at hearing the quick step behind him, and now stood hunched close to the door, his back turned to whatever visitor it might be. But Grizzel was long in opening these days, and it gave Abelard his chance.

"Fulbert," he said. His throat was dry, and he had to swallow to get out the word.

Fulbert turned reluctantly. He had not recognized the husky voice. But when he lifted his eyes, and saw the familiar amazing presence, his shrunken body strung taut as a striking adder. He opened his mouth, but though the lips moved, no words came. Only the tiny hands, grimy with dirt, reached out before him, thrusting the loathed bulk away. It was the sight of the small grimy hands that broke Abelard's heart, and gave him wisdom, though not for himself.

He stepped back a pace.

"Master Fulbert," he said humbly. "I have come to ask if you will give me your niece in marriage."

He did not know what he was going to say until he said it. But suddenly with the words it seemed to him that a great wind that had been blowing in his ears fell silent, and that he was filled with a clear shining, such as must come to a redeemed soul after death.

Fulbert was gazing at him, his hands no longer thrusting, but clasping and unclasping above his stained soutane. At last he spoke.

"Marriage?" he whispered. "Marriage?"

"In marriage," said Abelard gravely. So happy was he, so like a forgiven child, that he stood there smiling down at Fulbert, gentleness in his eyes. And suddenly Fulbert reached out his hands to him as a child might, crying loudly, unashamedly, a desperate crying that only knew the depth of its despair because it has begun to hope. Abelard was standing with his arm about him, supporting him, when Grizzel's bearded countenance came round the door. Still holding him he passed inside, and the door was shut.

CHAPTER II

It was very quiet in the wood: Abelard, following the bridle-path to Beaupréau, reined in for a moment at the edge of a clearing. The birds had been loud all morning after a night of rain, but now there was no sound from them, except for a single wood-pigeon. It must be long past noon. If he had not missed his way at starting, he would have been at Le Palais by now. As it was, he would be lucky to reach it before sundown, and he must read the Good Friday Office in the forest. Perhaps, he admitted wryly, it would be with more devotion than if Heloise were kneeling beside him.

He slid to the ground, and opening his saddlebag, got out his missal and a crust of bread. He stood beside the mare for a while, stroking her nose, and then opened the palm of his hand to the soft nuzzling lips. There was no reason why the beasts should fast, he thought, even though it were Good Friday: they had not betrayed their Maker. Though even as a small boy he had noted that the creatures seemed to keep Good Friday as devoutly as men did, though with no mourning, but a kind of small secret happiness. Never, as far as he could remember, had Good Friday been wild or cold, though he had shivered through many an Easter Sunday. But that day seemed halcyon, and even small things on the ground, budding briars and yellow gorse and the tiny fists of curling bracken, had a kind of radiance about them. Strange, the day that once began with darkness and ended with earthquake. Leaning with one arm flung across the mare, he began to read.

"*Come, and let us return unto the Lord: for he hath torn and he will heal us; he hath smitten and he will bind us up. After two days he will revive us: in the third day he will raise us up, and we shall live in his sight. Then shall we know, if we follow on to know the Lord: his going forth is prepared as the morning; and he shall come unto us as the rain, as the latter and former rain unto the earth.*

"*O Ephraim, what shall I do unto thee?*"—The proud head twisted round, the soft nozzle thrust between him and the missal, sniffing at it distrustfully. Abelard closed it and laid it down on the solid green cushion of the furze.

"There's nothing there for you, girl," he said fondly. "Try the green grass." He led her across the open sward to the low branch of an oak, tethered her, and came back to his book.

"*O Ephraim, what shall I do unto thee? O Judah, what shall I do unto thee? for your goodness is as a morning cloud, and as the early dew it goeth away. Therefore*

*have I hewed them by the prophets; I have slain them by
the words of my mouth."*

The words were at variance with the gentleness of the
day: they echoed the jarring note, like an owl's hoot, that
had marred his peace. For though the quiet exaltation
that had come upon him when first he spoke to Fulbert
had lasted with him all these days of his ride to Brittany,
it had been rudely shaken by Gilles. He had gone to see
him the morning after, full of his plans. Gilles listened
and said nothing.

"What do you think of it, Gilles?" he had asked, suddenly diffident.

"*Quem deus vult perdere,*" said Gilles, and would say
no more. Then when Abelard pressed him, "You are one
of the fools," he bit the words as he said them, "who
think that you can call back yesterday. You think words
can make all, and break all. Fulbert is mad, and now I
think you are as mad as he. Abelard, the married man—
there'll be fine songs about you now."

Abelard flushed. "He has promised to keep it secret.
He says he will be content if he alone and his kinsmen
know that she is my wife. He knows it would be the end
of all things for me. He has given me his word."

"He has given you his word?" said Gilles, dangerously
smooth. "That is a strong tower: the righteous runneth
into it, and is safe."

"He means to keep it. He swore it"—in spite of himself
his eyes began to twinkle and a laugh crept into his voice
—"on his relic, you know, the funny little knuckle of the
spine of St. Evroul, that he got from the King's chaplain."

Gilles looked at him sourly, but the candles had begun
to gleam in his eyes.

"Will you get out of my sight, Peter?" said he. "They say Providence has a care for children and fools, but I have small use for either."

His eyes were on his book again: he would not watch Abelard go. Abelard had reached the door: suddenly he turned and came back.

"You might give me your blessing, Gilles," he said soberly.

Gilles looked up at him. There was an odd look, almost of misery, in the small pigs' eyes.

"I have never cared much for anyone in all my life," he said irrelevantly, "and I have no mind to begin doing it at seventy. I will give you no blessing. I believe it would be better to wish you a broken neck than a happy end to your journey."

Abelard's jaw stiffened.

"Better a broken neck than broken faith, you'll say," went on Gilles. "You have had too much trade with words, Peter. But a man patches leather with leather and iron with iron. Now go. Take Heloise my greeting, and tell her I agree with every word she will say. And that's all you will get from me."

The mare was munching steadily, now and then blowing through its nostrils and shaking its head.

"*O Lord, I have heard thy speech, and was afraid; O Lord, revive thy work in the midst of the years, in the midst of the years make known; in wrath remember mercy.*"

Sadly Abelard read on.

"*O God, from whom Judas received the punishment of his guilt, and the good thief the reward of his confession: grant us the effect of thy clemency, that as our*"

Lord Jesus Christ, in his passion, gave to each a different
retribution, according to his desert, so he would deliver
us from our old sins, by grace of his resurrection; who
liveth."

It might not be repentance, his agony for Fulbert's
brief, but perhaps, on Good Friday, it might be counted
to him for desert. *By grace of his resurrection: who
liveth.* A small blue butterfly flickered past him, and lit
swaying on a tuft of flowering gorse. His heart leapt.

> "Now let us praise together
>   This earth that is new-stirred,
> And happy be the lover
>   Who knows his prayer is heard
>   By grace of Her
>   Whose altars—"

He stopped aghast. What blasphemy was this that he was
humming in the midst of the Passion? His mouth set. At
least he could lay this penance on himself. He would not
lie at Le Palais tonight. He would ride down now to
Beaupréau and say the *Tenebrae* with old Hervé the
priest, and watch the sepulcher till dawn. It would be
some small amends for that night of Holy Week, a year
ago, and his graceless memory now.

The level sunlight through the east window was shining red on Abelard's eyelids. He blinked and awoke. He
was lying on the floor beside the sepulcher where last
night he had helped old Hervé to carry the rough
wooden cross. Hervé himself was brushing the earthen
floor with a besom of twigs, busy and intent, looking,
with his short legs and rounded rear, like a small white

dog. Abelard sat up, bewildered. He must have fallen
asleep, and Hervé had covered him with his cloak.

"Why did you not waken me, Hervé?"

"Young things need their sleep," said Hervé placidly,
speaking from his eighty years. "You had a good inten-
tion, but you had ridden a many miles. Maybe, now
that you are wakened, you will say Prime with me? It is
not often I have company for it. But there's no hurry.
It's barely five o'clock."

Abelard stooped to pass under the lintel, and stepped
out into the early light. He stood leaning against the
door-post, and looked about him. The tiny church, with
buttresses shoring it up as big as itself, seemed so old
and overgrown that it might be a boulder fallen from
the hillside into the long green meadow that gave Beaupréau its name: it looked as ancient as the Druid stone,
sunk among the elder-bushes beside it. The moss on the
thatch was gold-green in the light: and under the eaves,
on a level almost with his head, a brooding swallow
looked at him with bright, indifferent eyes. There had
been heavy rain in the night—it had been a wet spring, he
had noted coming through the Loire country how many
pools caught the sky in the forest, and even in the open
fields. Here, a corner of the meadow was under water;
he crossed over to it, thinking to bathe his hands and
face, and hesitated, unwilling to break the surface of that
shallow world. Each small green blade stood up, distinct
and delicate in this strange medium of another element;
he saw the faint pink of the daisy-buds tight closed: and
farther away, where the ground sloped under the trees,
the white stems of the long grass gleamed in deeper but
still translucent stretches of quiet water. It was more

mysterious, he thought, than when one looks through shallow water at the bottom of a pond. This was the world he knew, but with another element added to it, not unclothed, but clothed upon, mortality swallowed up of life. Then he heard the old man calling him, and went back, stumbling at the downward step into the green gloom of the church, to kneel before the stripped altar with its empty tabernacle and unlit candles. Hervé kept by the old ways, he said: it was not till evening that he would make the fire outside with a flint on the great stone—some said it was a Druid stone, but it had kindled Christ's fire often enough since to sain it—and from that, light the candles on the altar and from them the whole parish would light its Easter fire.

It was still early, barely six o'clock, when Abelard turned to look back from the crest of the hills. The gray church looked more than ever like a rock, and the tiny parsonage no bigger than a beehive. He could see Hervé coming and going, spreading patches of white on the elder-bushes about the house: the altar-cloths, most likely, to have them white for tomorrow's feast. The Druid stone and the elder trees and the immemorial oaks: surely it must take a stout heart to live solitary amid the ancient wickedness: but then Hervé also was old, and the ancient wickedness seemed harmless enough that April morning.

For an hour or more the way led through the forest: then it skirted the side of a hill, with a great clump of yew trees climbing to the crest of it. Those yew trees were the landmark: hereafter Abelard would be riding on Le Palais land. He came out on the hill-top, and halted the mare: for a while he sat there, his hand shading his eyes.

Below him lay the wide plain, vineyard and tilth and pasture, shimmering with the warm sun upon the rain-wet earth, and from the misty distance that was Nantes the road from Nantes to Poitiers winding through it. It might have been quicker after all if he had kept the road to Nantes, he thought, instead of trying the short cut through the woods from Saumur: but he would rather have his forest vigil that was no vigil in the end, than spend the night at Nantes in the canons' lodging at St. Pierre.

His eye followed the road, with the blue glint of the Sèvre beside it for a while: then the smaller road that stuck off to the left, and ran through fields, most of them plowed: and so to a little huddle of gray roofs, like pebbles by a stream, and above them, on the only cliff for miles of level land, the ancient shabby keep. Never had he looked upon it so, coming from a great way off, and something moved in his breast like the fluttering of a bird's wing. *Quoniam advena sum et peregrinus:* of his own choice he came to it an alien and a stranger, he that might have lived and died there, and plowed and sown, and begotten many sons on Heloise. Well, he had chosen. Plato and Aristotle might be barren pastures, but so were the fields of the stars.

He had two ways before him: to go down the hillside to the plain, and ride through the vineyards till he struck the road that wound up through the village to the keep: the other, to keep left along the hills that ringed the plain till he dropped down on the bogland where the Sanguèze had its springs, where he and Guibert used to come for snipe. There was a bridle-track by the river all along the valley: he could follow it to the mill dam below the cliff, leave his horse at the mill and cross the stones at the ford, and climb the cart track, and so come upon her unawares, it might be in the orchard, feeding the chickens, like flecks of moving sunlight in the grass. His hand shook on the bridle, thinking of it: he pulled up the mare's head and turned her to the left. It was the longer way, but time was standing still for him. The world was like the pool in the green meadow: the clear water was far above his head.

So it was that he did come upon her unawares, but not in the orchard. Half a mile from the cliff above the river the valley widened and ran back into the hills, leaving a clear space like a triangle with the river at its base: it was full of hazel copses and willow, with little tracks among them that he and his brothers and how many generations before them had made, gathering wild strawberries in June, nutting in the wood smoke of brown October days. They had been faggoting here, he saw, but had not finished stacking them: the faggots lay here and there as they had been tied, strangely black against the quick green of the grass, and growing among them as though the sunlight had spilled itself, the primroses lay in drifts. He reined in the mare that he might look at it. Something older stirred in him than the movement of his heart at the sight of his ancient roof tree. He saw the faggots, dead in spring, with their promise of winter fires: the eternal rhythm of the seasons spoke to his blood: he saw the succession of life and death, and the hearth that gave life unto the world.

So when as it seemed to him his eyes were opened and

he saw her, it was with no surprise, with hardly a quicker beat of his pulse. How should she not be here, that was the stillness in the heart of flame, the beauty of all beauty? She had been kneeling, gathering primroses, and now moved out from the stack of faggots that had hidden her, but he had no thought for that, nor how it was that at first the valley had held all the promise of the earth but this, and then had flowered in her. She stood there, holding up her long green gown to make a lap for the flowers, her head bowed, gravely pondering. Have you gathered enough, O Beloved, for the woodland rides of the world? For in that green lap lies the seed of mortal beauty, the sap of ancient trees, the white flower of the thorn.

For a long moment, silence kept the valley. Then the mare, impatient to be home, pawed the soft ground and tossed her head with a jingling of the bit. At the sharp sound in that quiet place, Heloise raised her head, and saw a strange horseman on the track beside the stream. The light was in her eyes. She put up her hand to shade them, but in that moment he had leapt to the ground and was striding towards her, his cloak streaming behind him in the old remembered gesture. She did not move to meet him, because she could not: but as he came nearer he cried aloud, not to greet her, but at the glory that was in her face.

CHAPTER III

THE two men, Abelard and Hugh the Stranger, sat on for a while by the hearth after the women had gone to bed. No one, not even Heloise, had asked him what brought him to break his purpose, and come back to Le Palais before the summer. But it was a house where his comings and goings had never been questioned: as for Heloise, he judged that she had sufficient answer in her own heart. For himself, he was strangely loath to break the trance of peace that had held him all day. Paris and his lodging in the Maison du Poirier and the dark house in the Rue des Chantres had fallen illimitably far: they had nothing to do with this simpler, less complicated, less urgent world. Hugh asked him if he had noticed how far the plowing was on round Beaupréau, and if he had seen the way Hucbald was letting the rushes spoil his pasture; he had no care for the clogging of his drains. He had heard snipe drumming on the bog: now that the close season was over, Abelard and he might have a day or two's fishing, if he could stay. It was queer, said Hugh, how Lent and the close season for trout should so often overlap, but thank God tomorrow was Easter Day. If all had gone as it should, they would have been christening Denise's last tomorrow, but he had only breathed long enough to be baptized. Hugh crossed himself. Denise had fretted a while, but it was a mercy young Peter Astrolabe was on hands, and in the end she had taken him from his mother, for Heloise was growing thin with suckling that great boy. But I'm keeping you up,

[128]

Peter, he said, suddenly remembering, and stood up to go to bed. Abelard went with him through the solar, paused to say good-night to Denise lying half asleep with his son pudgy and comfortable on her accustomed arm, and opened the door that led from it to the stairway to the keep.

The great hall and the solar had been new built by his grandfather on the gentle western slope of the hill, and no one coming up the causeway that climbed to it from the village, over the drawbridge and into the green court-yard, would have dreamt that the eastern face broke in a shaggy cliff almost sheer to the river. But the keep up which Abelard was climbing was older far: they had built it out of the hillside almost as the cliff-swallows might, story after story hewn in part from the rock, and the battlements that crowned it were continued round the grassy mound of the cliff-top. Even in Berengar's time the three small rooms, one above the other, had been little used, unless for stores, the lower two for sacks of grain, the topmost for a kind of armory: and when Abelard had made the demand, unheard of for a youngster of twelve, that he might have it for himself, instead of sleeping with his brothers in the great hall-bed, as comfortable as a basket of puppies, the household thought the boy was bewitched. But Berengar was an indulgent father: he had the carpenter make him a box bed and a table and a great chest. The windows in the four-foot walls were no wider than arrow-slits, but the landscape glimpsed through them had a queer wizard quality of remoteness, and above all the stairway led up a few steps into that walled and grassy place, a natural rampart that no one could reach unless by his consent, and that was

a well of sunlight all the summer long. Not even the
bleakest January nights could drive him from his eyrie
to the frowsty warmth of his brothers' bed; and even
when he came back, a distinguished stranger, he had been
firm in refusing the state-bed for visitors in the solar,
beside the master's bed where Denise and her husband
slept. It was to his eyrie that he had brought Heloise,
and there she had slept till in November Denise had refused to allow her to go any longer up and down the
dark uncertain steps. For the boy's sake, she had stayed
down for the winter with Denise, but now that he was
taken from her she had gone back to sleep among the
battered shields and boar spears. The walled grassy space
high under heaven had the same enchantment for her as
for Abelard: she would sit there with Peter Astrolabe by
the hour, exulting that even the wheeling pigeons would
not come so far.

So, when Abelard reached the topmost stair and felt
rather than saw that the room was empty, he knew where
he would find her. But for a moment he hesitated, standing in the dark. Confident as he had been all the long days
of riding, and steady as his purpose was, he had a mis-
giving that he could not understand. Would Heloise feel
as he did, or rather, as he had, for the peace of this day
had in some queer way shaken that earlier, stranger
peace? He would gladly put it off till the morning, if he
could: but he had felt before the day was ended that she
was aware of some undercurrent in him. He straightened
his shoulders, and climbed out under the open sky.

She had been watching for him, puzzled by the long
wait in the empty room below, and was about to rise to
come down to him when the dark figure suddenly loomed

up between her and the stars. Abelard heard the little
catch in her breath, and all the trouble of his errand was
forgotten in a surge of tenderness that brought him to the
ground beside her, his arms about her knees. She stooped
over him, holding his head so tightly in her hands as
almost to hurt him. Then, relaxing with a long sigh of
content, she sat back; he knelt beside her, his arms about
her body, his head against her shoulder, and she gathered
the folds of her cloak about them both.

For a long time they sat, unwilling to speak or move,
their mood as quiet as the April night. Then suddenly
Heloise spoke, her voice cracking a little.

"Abelard, I cannot bear to ask you, but it is tearing at
me. When must you go?"

"The day after tomorrow, little heart." His arms
tightened about her as he felt her quiver. "But—" he
hesitated, and plunged, "I shall take you with me."

"With you!" It was a cry of pure ecstasy. She thrust
him away from her, to look at his face, laughter bubbling
in her throat. Then she grew suddenly grave. "But, dearest, how? What could you do with me?"

"It is going to be all different, Heloise. Before I came
away, I went to see your uncle." He felt an uncontrol-
lable shiver go through her, and again his arm tightened
about her. "Dearest, he will not touch you. He will never
touch you again. Heloise, your heart would break for
him if you saw him, he is so little and broken and old."

He got to his feet. It was being unbelievably difficult.

"I saw him one day." But how could he tell her, how
make her see the agony that had shown him all men's
agony: he could hardly remember it now himself: it was
a thing that might have happened to another man.

"I had been reading. I was thinking about you. And I saw him from the window, so shabby, not looking at anyone, hurrying to get home. I could not bear it. And I went after him and he tried to push me away. His hands . . . And I asked him if it would make it better if I married you."

He turned at the further end of the parapet to look at her. She was sitting quite still, her eyes fixed straight before her. Yet even in the faint light he recognized the look that was in them. He had seen it before, the same attitude, the same stare; it was when he looked back from kneeling beside Fulbert, with the candle rolling, still burning, on the floor.

"Heloise," he came across to her, the words tumbling from him, "you must not look like that. You must listen to me." He was stooping over her, he had caught her arms, almost shaking her. "What is there to be afraid of? Fulbert—if you had seen him. Oh, my dear, he cried with happiness. And I—I was so happy too." His voice broke in spite of himself; he looked like a bewildered child.

A little sound broke from Heloise, half laugh, half sob. She caught him to her. "Oh, my little one," she said, crushing his cheek against hers. "Oh, my little one," and for a moment she crooned over him, still laughing, but her tears hot on his face. Then suddenly she sat up and held him away from her.

"Dear, I am sorry. I will be reasonable. Sit down, or walk up and down if you like, and tell me about it."

He stood up with a relieved shake of his shoulders, like a retriever come to land.

"Well . . . there isn't much more to tell. Somehow, it all seemed easy, after that. I said I would come here for you, and bring you back with me, secretly, and you would be with him, just as if you had never been away. And then we would get married, and you would go on living with him, just as you used to. Only that he will let us see each other as much as we like."

There was a silence for a while. It did not sound to Abelard so credible as before.

"Do you remember Evrard and his housekeeper?" said Heloise, almost casually.

Abelard flushed. "That was different. That— But I forgot to tell you. Fulbert promised—he gave me his oath— that he would keep our marriage a secret. It is only for his own peace of mind. He does not care about anything else if he knows that we are married and not—not living in sin. He does love you, Heloise," he ended wistfully.

"I know. He did." The edge of bitterness had gone from her voice and left it toneless. "But—you do not understand, Abelard. You did not live with him for months and months after . . . after he knew. He—it isn't the same man. We killed him, that night. And now something else walks about in his dead body." She was shivering, but her voice was steady enough. "Sometimes the old Fulbert comes back. That was what made it so terrible. But it was a ghost coming back. The string is broken. Only, if a hand it knows touches it—" She ended in a little moan.

"But, Heloise, if you had seen him. He put his arms round me and kissed me, when I was coming away. And he took his oath as solemnly as if it were on the Host. He does not want to ruin me. I could swear he does not. And he knows it would ruin me if—if this were known."

She shook her head. "Abelard, you do not know the

power you have over people. When you are with him,
he is what you think him to be, gentle and magnanimous,
and old. But I know. Gilles knows, ask Gilles. He is mad.
Did you," her voice was suddenly eager, "did you tell
Gilles?"

"I did."

"What did he say?"

"He said, *Quem deus vult perdere*. He said too," Abelard was determined to be honest, " 'Give Heloise my
greeting, and tell her I agree with everything she says.' "

Heloise made no comment. Suddenly she rose, and
going across to him, put her hands on his shoulders and
looked into his face.

"Abelard, will you listen to me, and not think I am
putting my will against yours? Not think that I am only
a woman talking? No, do not kiss me. Not yet."

"Beloved, could I ever think you only a woman talking?"

Heloise was looking over his shoulder, as if she heard
an echo from some forgotten sunny morning of childish
grief. *And the day will come when I am no more Heloise
but just a woman*—and then she had heard Abelard's foot
on the stair. She drew her mind away.

"Listen, Abelard. It is not a question of whether or
not Fulbert will keep his word, and keep our marriage
secret. I know he will not. But this is what matters, that
you should do a thing that will put it in his power to
ruin you—do a thing that would be your ruin, if he, or
anyone else, chose to say it aloud."

Abelard moved restlessly. "You speak as if marriage
were adultery."

"It is a kind of adultery," said Heloise, "for you."

[134]

He looked at her, mutely questioning. here was no moment for quick answers.

"I know what you could say, you could say that marriage is a sacrament. I do not know. Perhaps it is for a layman. But it is not a sacrament for you. I cannot tell you, cannot explain to you, what I mean. I cannot explain it to myself. It is not only that you would be breaking faith with the Church, it is breaking faith with something you pledged yourself to, long before you were tonsured, or took the canon's vows: the *Civitas Dei*, only it is wider than Augustine's—Plato would know, and Socrates—it's the spirits of just men made perfect, a kind of community of noble souls." She stopped, breathless.

He looked down at her, worshiping, but honestly perplexed.

"But, Heloise, if this is true, I break faith—and I know I break faith—every time I take you in my arms."

She looked at him fearlessly. "I know you do. I know that we are living in what the Church calls fornication and uncleanness, even if to me it has burnt up heaven and earth into such a glory that I cry out to God in an adoration for it, when I should be on my knees repenting it. And I know they are wrong, St. Paul or St. James or whoever it was. And yet I know, I feel in my heart that they were right."

Still he did not speak.

"But I have accepted that. If—if it had been different, if you had not been sworn to a diviner thing, I might have married you and gone on my knees for the blessing of the Church, and felt our nuptial Mass was not a lie. But I know that this is our sin, which is also our glory.

And what we must not do is to pretend that it is not a sin, and sprinkle it with holy water and cover it up with holy words, until it rots us."

He stopped her then.

"Heloise, you do not know. You never knew your father and mother. You were brought up in a convent, and then by an old man, among churchmen. If you had known my father—but think even of Denise."

There broke from her a little wailing cry. "Ah, if we only could, if we only could." She buried her face in his breast.

He took her in his arms. "But, little love, we can. Why should we not live as happy as they do?"

She sprang away from him. "Because we cannot. Because we must hide and lie, and lie and hide. And even then it will be of no use, and the truth will come out and I shall have smirched the proudest name in Christendom. Do you think I have not heard what they say? Do you think I have not read what the Fathers have said about women—what men have said about women—since the beginning of the world? Do you think it is easy for a woman to read over and over again that she is a man's perdition? Oh, my love, were there ever two great lovers, but they ended in sorrow?"

"But, Heloise, what of your name? You that talk of smirching mine?"

She looked at him a little while without speaking.

"Beloved, do you not know that I would rather be called your harlot than be empress of Christendom?"

He dropped on his knees at her feet, hiding his face in her dress.

"But," she went on, "you must let me choose. I want

[136]

nothing from you but you. I will have you bound by no bond but your love only. I am not ashamed to be called your harlot. I would be ashamed to be called your wife. I shall do you no harm as your harlot. They'll only laugh a little and sing the *Chanson d'Aristote:* and now that I am away here in Brittany, they will forget. And I know —I know already how much better it is for your work that you see me seldom. Sometimes," her voice shook, "you will come here, and we shall still be happy. Think of this morning. And if it is agony, your going away, I sometimes think that perhaps God will let it be our expiation for whatever is unlawful in our joy."

For a long time neither spoke: he knelt, his face still hidden, her hand touching his hair. Bewildered, half-convinced by her wild logic, shaken to the soul by her amazing generosity, he had no words. His mind went round and round the weary circle. But of one thing only he was sure: that when he had given his word to Fulbert to marry Heloise, he had known it was the one thing he must do. How grievously he had sinned against the Church or Heloise or himself, he did not know: but as to the quality of his sin against Fulbert he had no illusion: it was the supreme betrayal. While Heloise spoke, he had seen the world under lightning flashes of glory and terror, but not this plain sin between man and man. He had betrayed the house that sheltered him: he had played on the credulous affection of an innocent garrulous old man. For the sin of his flesh he would stand up and take whatever punishment God was pleased to send him, but this he could not face. He was Berengar's son: and he had failed in the point of honor.

He got to his feet, and drew her over to her seat against

the parapet. He could feel her trembling with exhaustion and reaction, and he himself was deadly weary, but they must make an end this night, if it killed them.

"Will you listen to me, beloved?" he began, speaking very quiet and low. "You will not let me take you in marriage. Secret or open, you say it is a sin: secret or open, you say it will destroy me. By this time I think my enemies have found that it is hard to destroy me. At any rate, whether our marriage is kept a secret or whether it is blazoned on the housetops, I know that I must have no more thought of high place in the Church. I shall not live a lie to myself. But, if Fulbert keeps his word, in a few years I shall have made myself such a name in Europe that an open avowal of my marriage will not even mist my fame. And whether he keeps his word or not, I must keep mine."

Heloise had been listening with drooped head and half-closed eyes, but at the sudden ring in his voice she looked up startled. For the first time she was seeing him, neither lover nor scholar nor master of debate, but the son of an ancient Breton house. That was what Gilles meant when he called him the Palatine.

"How God looks upon our sins together, I am too be-wildered to think, for I ask myself how can that be evil when all the good that is in me is bound up with my love of you. If it is evil, there is penance for it. But one thing I have done, and there is no penance for it. Think-ing by myself alone, away from you, I saw that I had done a thing for which a heathen Saracen would spit at me. I betrayed the man whose bread I had eaten. You were his ward: he trusted you to me, and I defiled you, eating at his table and sleeping under his roof. I wounded his honor, but I wounded my own, nigh to death."

Still she was silent.

"Do you not see, beloved?" he went on, troubled. "It is not only between you and me. It is between me and him. And I have given him my word."

She raised her head at that. "I do see," she said. "There is nobody in the whole world for me but you. I would go after you through the fires of Hell. I would lie and cheat for you, as I have lied and cheated already. I have given my honor to the carrion crows of Paris and been proud to be called your whore. But you—but you—" She broke into terrible weeping.

Bewildered, helpless, he gathered her into his arms. For a moment she struggled against him, then as desperately clung to him, shaking him as well as herself with the agony of her grief. He was powerless to comfort her: and when at last its violence was abated, she lay spent in his arms, now and then heaving a great sigh.

"Beloved"—he bent over her—"what can I do or say?"

She shook her head, and lifted one hand to touch his cheek.

"There is only one thing left," she said. "The grief that is to come will be no less than the love that went before it."

He shuddered at it, and in quick pity for him, she turned and flung her arms about him. For a while he sat, his cheek against hers: then, lifting her, carried her down the steps to their bed. Deadly weary as they were, they lay clinging to one another, like children in the dark, broken-hearted for each other, yet finding in the closeness and nearness of their bodies such consolation as might redeem all sorrows they had felt. Let the future bring what it might, thought Abelard, before he slept, if it left them the solace of each other's arms.

CHAPTER IV

THE Easter Mass was ended. Heloise, kneeling beside Denise, had listened to her lover's voice triumphant in the *Victimae Paschali*,

.

"*Dux vitae mortuus regnat vivus*,"

transcending and yet carrying with it the sparrow chirping of the little choir-boys, who stared at him round-eyed, worshiping. That he who was so nearly their lord should take his place surpliced among them seemed to them a more stupendous condescension than any unintelligible Incarnation. Through the east window Heloise saw a budded lime tree, holding up its small translucent cups of light: and her heart rose with it. From the moment she had wakened that morning with the west wind breathing on their faces through the open doorway, the doom and terror of the night had seemed only a bad dream: his arm was under her head. "*Pour forth upon us, O Lord, the spirit of thy love, that by thy loving kindness thou mayest make to be of one mind those whom thou hast fed with the sacraments of thine Easter.*" She was of one mind with him: come what might, she was content to go his way.

She stood by the well in the courtyard, waiting for him. Denise had left her to go into the bakehouse, where ever since daybreak there had been a cheerful clatter of tongues and the crackling of sticks under the great oven, in preparation for the Easter feast. Heloise would have followed her, but Denise refused.

"Child, there's plenty here to get under my feet without you. Wait for Peter. Let him have his day."

She saw him now, coming up the causeway, side by side with Hugh the Stranger in companionable silence. Then Hugh turned and went into the stable, and Abelard came towards her.

"Let's go down to the river," he said. He looked at her, a little discontented with the white coif that hid her hair. "Heloise, do you know that I have never done what all the lovers do, made you a spring garland? Do you know that until now we have wasted all our spring in a town?"

"If you knew how I have wanted you," said Heloise, "these April dusks in the fields." They had gone through the gate, and were going down the uneven track to the ford. "And yet the pain of it seemed the richest thing I have ever had."

"Amore crucior,
vulnere morior,
quo glorior,"

said Abelard under his breath. "Do you know the garland I am going to make you, Heloise? I was thinking of it this morning, before you wakened. If it were May, I thought it would be wild roses. I do not know why, but it must have a thorn in it. The wild roses were all over when we were riding down to Brittany last July. And then I looked at your dark hair and the small white face sleeping there, and I knew what it would be. First I shall plait you a crown of green rushes, so that I can fasten the twigs in

it and not hurt you: and then it will be *Flos de spina,*
flower of the thorn."

He reached up and pulled a branch from the blackthorn
hedge that overhung the track.

"It has always seemed to me the world's miracle," he
went on, touching the frail white blossom on the long
fierce spine. "I wonder what Adam thought his first
March day outside Paradise, when the thorns that had
cursed him all winter broke into anything so small and
white and tender as this."

"Peter? Are you there?"

The call came muffled from the hill behind them. They
stopped, reluctantly. Heloise shook her head at the truant
look preparing in Abelard's eyes.

"It's Hugh, and he sounds uneasy," she said. "We had
better go back." They turned, but stood aside to let the
slow cows go by on their way from their belated milking
to the water-meadow. They blew sweet breaths as they
went by, and one timid young heifer at the unaccustomed
sight of Abelard hustled into the hedge, throwing her
head over another's flank and looking at him with wild
frightened eyes.

"Chè, Chè," said Abelard comfortingly. The eyes
ceased to roll, though they still looked anxious, and she
swerved past him, cantering. The last laggard was coming through the gate as they reached it, and saw Hugh
the Stranger standing in the stable door.

"I wish you would look at the mare, Peter, if you are
going to ride her tomorrow. She won't let me near her.
Did you notice her lame yesterday?"

"I did not," said Abelard. "But then I was leading her
and walking slow with Heloise the last half-mile. Maybe

[142]

she picked up a thorn at the gap. Let me see, girl." The mare rubbed her head against his shoulder, and stood still while he lifted her fore foot.

"That's what it is, and a wicked one, too. I'll need to bathe it. Wait for me in the orchard, Heloise."

She went to the corn bin by the door and filled her lap, screwing up her eyes as she came from the pungent darkness into the naked sunlight of the court. Then the pigeons spied her and were on her with a swoop, settling on her shoulders and arms, and she flung them off, throwing the corn into the air like golden spray, and they rose after it, a fountain of white breasts and dazzling wings. One handful she kept for a brooding hen that she had found with some pride in a hollow tree in the orchard: but when she passed through the gate and came stooping under the low apple boughs that caught her hair and shook their strange cold dew upon her, she saw that someone was before her. Denise was kneeling beside the prisoner, lifting the grain and letting it fall again to tempt her, and making small crooning noises: and at last the hen replied, though querulously, lumbered with caution off her sitting of brown eggs and began to peck, grudgingly at first, then suddenly ravenous. Heloise, hidden among the apple boughs, stood watching: she was never weary of watching Denise. It was her patience, not holy like the conscious patience of the saints, offering up all vexation as a mortification, but a kind of natural wisdom: like the verse in Isaiah "and shall gently lead those that are with young." She could be brisk enough with anything that could run about, on two or four feet, but with Peter Astrolabe, or a blind puppy, or a beast that was near its time, she seemed never to grow weary. She stood up now, deep-breasted but still slender; "crossed beauty," they called her in that country, for she had brown eyes set far apart under hair that was very fair; then stooping, the hen now safely absorbed, she caught up an egg from the nest and held it to her ear, listening for the first faint tapping within. She looked up, a little guilty, as Heloise came across the dappled grass.

"It wasn't that I thought you would forget her," she said. "But I thought I would see if any of the eggs are chipped. They should be, any day now. And I did want you to have your one day with Peter."

"He is with Hugh in the stable. Hugh wanted him about the mare."

"Listen," said Denise. She held the brown shell to the girl's ear. It was there, the ghost of a voice, talking to itself in the dark. "And they have to work so hard to get out, the creatures." She looked down at the nest, the same humorous gentleness in her eyes as Heloise had seen, watching the youngsters busy with their bowls and spoons. "Look at them, Heloise," she said once, "trying so hard to live."

"Now, old woman," she pushed a platter of water under the greedy beak, "it's time you had a drink and got back to your work."

"Denise," said Heloise suddenly. "Abelard says he is taking me back with him tomorrow."

"I thought that would be the way of it," said Denise, rising to her feet. "I just thought that was what brought him back so soon. They can never let one be." Then her brow puckered. "But, child, what is he going to do with you? It would be a scandal if he had you to live

[144]

with himself, and he would never let you go back to your uncle."

"He says it will all be different," said Heloise mechanically. It seemed to her that she could do nothing but repeat what Abelard had said last night, and that was bald enough. "He wants to marry me."

Denise caught her breath. Her arms came about Heloise in one of her rare quick caresses.

"It is what I have prayed for," said she, "ever since I saw Hugh lifting you down from your horse that first night. Oh, my dear," her face had flushed and her eyes were bright with tears, "it is like when my father said that I might marry Hugh."

"But, Denise," Heloise stopped. She felt she must make Denise realize something of the issues: but do what she would, she could not revive her own conviction of last night. There was no power of thought left in her: nothing but the tranquil acceptance of this shining day.

"What is it, child? What is there to hinder you?"

"It is Abelard," said Heloise. "He is a clerk. If he marries me, it is the end of any great place for him."

"I never could see Peter a bishop," said Denise indifferently. "But if he wanted it, I expect they would make him one. You do not know Peter, child, the way I do. He has always got what he wanted, ever since he was the height of a turf."

"It is not only that," said Heloise. "But it would ruin him in Paris, if it were known. They might take the Schools from him."

"My dear, wherever Peter is, there the Schools will be. He emptied Paris once, and if they turn him out, he'll empty it again."

[145]

Heloise was silent. In spite of herself, her spirits rose.
I suppose, she thought to herself a little ruefully, even
one's lover can never seem quite so omnipotent as one's
eldest brother.

"But, Denise, do you not think it is wrong of him to
marry?"

The hen had gone clucking back to her nest. Denise
stooped to prop up the dilapidated osier basket that
stopped the hole.

"I think," she said painfully, "it would be wrong of
him not to. My dear," she turned to Heloise, her face
crimson, "you know what I did myself when I was a
girl, with Hugh. A whole summer through. And I'd have
gone after him begging through the ditches, if my father
had turned him away. And I wasn't ashamed of what I
had done. At least, I wasn't in my heart. And yet, once I
was married to him—it is like drinking when one is thirsty,
and yet you feel more blessed if you stop to say a *Benedicat* over it. I think, maybe, the difference was that now
I could say my prayers before I went to bed with him.
I couldn't before. It seemed like cheating."

Heloise was fingering the moss on the elm. "You see,
Denise," she said slowly, "I don't say any prayers, unless
for him. So it does not matter."

Denise held her peace. She knew the spirit in those
gray eyes was beyond her. She could not even fear for
a creature so fearless for itself.

"And I don't think," Heloise went on, "that he is doing it because he thinks it was wrong. It is because he
says he broke faith. It—it is the point of honor."

Denise lifted her hands and dropped them again. "That
is like him. They will never make a churchman out of

[146]

Peter. He is far more of a fighter than Guillaume, even though he would never do his service and be knighted. All these tussles of his, I sometimes think it is only the fun of unhorsing people, only in a different way. There he is. Look at him."

Abelard had vaulted the orchard gate without waiting to open it. Smiling and mischievous, he came across the grass, then suddenly halted, his arms resting on a branch, his eyes fixed on them. Standing there as they did, side by side, with the budding apple boughs above their heads, their faces turned to watch him, he felt suddenly remote, walled out from their mysterious ancient understanding. It was no altar-piece that he saw: it was an older thing than Mary the mother of Our Lord, and Anne the mother of Mary. It was Demeter and Persephone, with Pluto come to claim her, the six months ended. Then Heloise came a step to meet him, and the vision broke. He came gravely towards them, put his arm about her with a quick straining of her to his side, and then stood, looking down at his sister.

"Well? Will you give us your blessing, Denise?"

She looked up at him, her eyes soft, and for a while said nothing. Then she put her arms round his neck and kissed him. "I wish it could have been here," she said, complaining. "I'd have liked to spread your marriage-bed. Could you not leave her till the summer, Peter?"

He shook his head. "I promised to bring her back with me. The old man is breaking his heart for her, and I think he could not be content unless he saw her married with his own eyes. But now that I think of it, I must get her into Paris by stealth. Have you kept the nun's habit you came in, Heloise?"

[147]

"It is in my own chest," said Denise. "No, child, stay where you are. I'll bring it here to you. It will maybe need airing."

They moved into a patch of sunlight where an elm lay, half uprooted. Tiny sprigs of green were growing on the dark and ancient bark. Heloise touched them. It was like this morning, after last night's despair.

"Have you told Hugh?" she asked, after a while.

Abelard nodded.

"Did he say anything?"

"I said I was taking you with me to Paris, to marry you. And he said," Abelard's voice was grave, but his glance at her was side-long, " 'Man, I'm glad to hear it. But at that rate, I'll need to get her little horse in off the grass.' "

Denise heard them laughing as she came through the trees, her arms full of creased black draperies. They smelt fusty as she shook them out, and Abelard looked at them with distaste against the delicate lilac of her gown.

"Slip them on, Heloise," she said, "You are taller since you came, and we'll maybe have to let down the hem."

The girl stood up obediently, and Denise gathered up the dingy folds to slip them over her head. Suddenly, her face already hidden in them, she screamed aloud, thrusting them up with her hands.

"I can't, I can't," she cried, struggling with the black folds already fallen about her arms, and growing more hopelessly entangled. Even when Denise had pulled her free of them, she stood there shaking and crying, her hands over her eyes, more like a frightened child than Denise had ever seen her.

"There," she said, putting her warm hands on the girl's

[148]

shoulders, and holding her. "There. It's all right now. Child, you're like a little pony that has seen a ghost at the side of the road."

Heloise nodded. She stood, trying to twist the quivering of her mouth into a smile. "I am sorry," she said shakily. "I think—I think I felt rather like a pony. A pony that has seen its own ghost. I suppose it was what Soeur Godric used to say at Argenteuil, that she knew someone was walking over her grave."

"They're ugly things, anyhow," said Denise comfortably, stirring the tumbled heap with her foot. "And come to think of it, I'd as soon put a young bride into her shroud as into these. I'll find something else will hide you just as well."

"Denise," said Abelard diffidently, "you haven't a suit of young Berengar's? Surely she is about his height."

"To be sure I have," said Denise. "There's one he left behind him—you remember, Heloise, at Hallowe'en, when he came home from his uncle's at Clisson. He had grown too broad in the shoulders for it, though it was new when he went away. You can try it on after dinner. But you'll do no more till you have some food in you. There's the children back from catechism."

She bundled the nun's habit under her arm and went down the orchard. Abelard stood a moment, looking down at Heloise.

"Will you be Berengar, beloved," he said softly, "and ride to Paris to the Schools with your uncle Peter?"

She looked up at him, her eyes alight. They walked together on the daisied grass, where the shadows of the apple boughs made a stiff mosaic beneath their feet, and

Abelard saw the woods through which tomorrow would find them riding, he and she.

"Beloved," he stopped and set his hands on her shoulders, "do you know what this will mean? If you are Berengar, you need have no woman with you. Guibert is in Paris. And for the first time in our lives, you and I will be alone."

It was barely sunrise when the two rode over the drawbridge and down the causeway; the morning ghost of the Easter moon lay on its back over the keep. Abelard was determined to start early, that they might be clear of the plain before the mid-day heat. They would avoid Nantes, he had decided, Nantes, and Angers, and Le Mans, though that was the shorter road. He was too familiar a figure on it. Instead, he would keep south of the Loire, through the woods past Azay and Chinon to Tours, and north from Tours to Chartres, and so to Paris. The slight figure still muffled in its cloak was very quiet, and he had the wisdom to keep silence for a while. Coming back through the solar for the cloak he had forgotten in the keep, he had seen her standing in her boy's clothes beside Denise's great bed, empty only for a tiny heave of the bedclothes at the further side. She was not crying, only rigid. He had gone back into the hall to talk to Hugh the Stranger till she came out.

The village was still only half awake: here and there the creak of a well-rope, or the sharp smell of newly-kindled wood. But the mists were rising, and soon the sun was warm enough for Heloise to get rid of her cloak. They halted while he dismounted to fold it and strap it

to his own saddle: and suddenly it seemed to him that all
the grief of the parting was folded up with the cloak, for
she straightened her shoulders and cantered ahead, and
by the time he came galloping behind her, it was a boy's
face that provoked him, over her shoulder. The smell of
the sweet warm grass steeped their bodies through: and
when they rode through a lane of crimson hawthorn, he
remembered with a tide of rising exaltation that two days
from now would be the first of May. They would keep
their Vigil of Venus in the woods. What was there in
love that it taught a man all the mysteries of the ancient
faiths? He looked at the young creature riding ahead of
him, with a kind of awe. Was this the Heloise he knew,
or had Psyche become Eros, and was he riding with Love
himself?

The weather held. It was seven days instead of three
before they reined in their horses and sat, their eyes
dazzled at the silver of the Loire at Tours: and if Abelard
closed his mind to the memory of Paris and the turbulent
crowds of his scholars shouting poor Ralph of Beauvais
down, he had good reason for it. The days of riding between Paris and the west he had always counted as singularly his own: he was responsible to no one but himself,
he felt, and sometimes he would stop in open country
and think exultingly that no one in the world, for Guibert mattered no more than his own shadow, could be
certain where he was, or lay any claim upon him: he was
absolute master of himself. But now, with the madness of
May in his blood, and Heloise transmuted in the preg-
nant stillness of the woods into some wild changeling of
laughter and sudden passion, it seemed to him that he was
master of space and time. They would halt at a village

to buy food, and now and then the two would stop for a meal at a parsonage, and Heloise would carry herself as meek as a shy lad riding to the Schools at the heels of his distinguished uncle: the two would play the whole comedy of timid submission on one side and indulgent sternness on the other, but they soon wearied of it, and could not ride too quickly till the woods again received them into their sun-charmed world. The April rains had left the valley of the Loire bewitched between wood and water: he would lay her in a forest pool to see how golden she was in the brown water, and carry her from it to worship her whiteness on the grass. Their minds burnt with love as their bodies with the sun, they hardly felt the chill shadow of the walls of the Abbey as they rode past Charlemagne's tower. But when they turned into the Rue de la Scellerie and on to their hostelry under the shadow of St. Gatien, their hearts misgave them. They would ride east no more. Tomorrow they must take the northern road, to Paris.

They slept ill. Their upper room in the hostelry was small, and full of stenches after their forest nights. They would have been better in the guesthouse at St. Martin's, Abelard said, but he had shirked the hospitable commotion that his coming would have roused, and the friendly inquisition his nephew would have to face. Heloise turned and tossed and saw the window darken and grow gray again before she slept: and it seemed to her she had only closed her eyes when Abelard's hands were touching her to waken her. She opened her eyes and looked up at him: but her broken cry of recognition had a poignancy he did not understand. The face looking down at her was

no longer the face of the forest god, but the haggard
scholar who had been her lover first: and it seemed to her
that her heart clave to him, as it had not to the other.

He sat down beside her on the bed, looking at her remorsefully. He was fully dressed.

"I am a brute to wake you, Heloise. But there is a man
I want to hear, lecturing at the Cathedral Schools at six.
I'd have let you sleep and gone myself, but I did not like
the look of them downstairs last night, and I do not want
you sleeping here alone. Will you get up and come with
me?"

She was already pulling on Berengar's hose. He sat
contentedly, munching an apple, watching her dress.

"Who is he, Peter?"

"Bernard Sylvestris. They don't talk much of him at
Paris yet, but I heard Hildebert speak about him when I
rode through Le Mans a week ago. Very young, but as
wise as a troll, they say: one of the small dark men that
were left over from the first race. Hildebert says he is a
poet. And Hildebert should be a judge."

"Where does he come from?"

"No one knows. Except that he is a Breton. Some say
he is from Carnac or Locmariaquer. Anyhow, they say
he is like something would come out of a wood, and that
that is why he was nicknamed Sylvestris. It is his great
word for the primal chaos, *antiqua silva*, the ancient
wood. Ready? There's the bell."

She pulled the hood of her cloak about her head, and
they went down the steep stair and out through the court-
yard into the Place in front of the cathedral. For a moment they walked in the strange argent light that filled the
square as though Tours itself lay beneath the silver water

of the Loire: then Abelard turned in at the side of the cathedral, as the last vibration of the great bell died. An aged canon, a pace or two before them, was going down the paved walk to the north door, seemingly to early Mass. Abelard halted in his quick stride.

"Don't overtake him," he murmured. "I believe it is Roscelin."

The old man had reached the steps. He turned and looked back, a bitter withered face, unshaven, with reddish eyebrows going white. He had the air of a very ancient fox slinking home to his covert in the early morning. A spark of recognition gleamed in his eyes, and he came back a step or two to meet them.

"If it is not a phantasma of the morning," he said in the high elaborate voice of the old rhetorician, "I should say it was my one-time pupil, Peter Abelard."

"You are too good a nominalist to see phantasmata, Master Roscelin," said Abelard courteously. "You are well?"

"I am old," said Roscelin. "But I have my eyes. Though indeed I do not think I have set them on you since you were the height of the lad that is lurking behind you." A glance like a barb shot at Heloise, who had fallen back a step in due respect. "But Tours is honored: what brings you so far from Paris, Master Peter?"

"My private affairs," said Abelard, so pleasantly that it was a moment before the rebuff went home. "And I am now on my way to hear your new Master of the Schools. Hildebert tells me he is as good a Platonist as Bernard of Chartres." He made to turn towards the cloister, down which two belated scholars were hurrying.

As Abelard spoke, the crafty eyes were perpetually

[154]

sliding towards Heloise, who stood meekly waiting, her face downcast and partly hidden by Berengar's hood.

"And Ganymede goes with you?" He stooped forward smiling, to look under the hood.

Heloise smiled back, and raised her head, shy and pleased to be taken notice of. "But my name is not Ganymede, Master Roscelin," she said, in a piping treble. "My name is Berengar, sister's son to my uncle Peter."

The eyes slid from one to the other. "Well, have a care of him, Master Peter," said Roscelin. "It is a tender youth to be let loose in the streets of Paris."

Abelard bowed. "He is in my charge," he said quietly. "And now I shall take my leave of you, Master Roscelin, or I shall be showing small courtesy to Sylvestris. Come, boy." He swung her round, with no gentle hand, and turned down the cloister, his hand still gripping her shoulder. Roscelin stood looking after them. He was smiling a small secret smile.

They were late. The long vaulted room was crowded, but there was a narrow ledge on one side the embrasure of the door. Abelard set Heloise upon it and stood beside her, half hidden in the shadow. From the cathedra at the further end a low oddly resonant voice was speaking, half chanting. No one had turned to stare at their incoming. Abelard made mental note of it. It was an orator who could so hold his men at six o'clock in the morning.

It was some little time before he himself paid much heed. The encounter with Roscelin had shaken him with one of his swift deadly angers. Ganymede: lurking: so the world looked to a fox, and sure enough, he left the fox's smell behind him. But gradually the strange voice had its way with him, lulling him the more for the half-unfamiliar Breton accent of the Latin, and the singing note, alternating between verse and prose. Broceliande, he was saying, and the woods of the Ardennes, and Italian Silo, that sees from its high pines the white sails of twin seas. What kind of wizard was the little man, that when he spoke you saw what he saw, yet on those white sails neither your eyes nor his had ever rested? It was rivers now, the waters of Shiloh that go softly, the Tiber that bears Rome upon his shoulders, the Po that rolls towards Venice its imperious way. And now it was the stars. This must be the poem of which Hildebert had spoken, the making of the world from chaos and old night: and still the little figure swung there, gazing out under a penthouse of great brows and a thatch of black hair, his short-sighted eyes rapt and unaware, unless of the vision within.

He had halted. The rhythm changed into prose, yet if anything more resonant, thought Abelard, than his verse.

"Perfect from the perfect, beautiful from the beautiful, eternal from the eternal: from the intellectual world the sensible world was born: full was that which bore it, and its plenitude fashioned it full." Since John Scotus Erigena, said Abelard to himself, there has been no philosopher who was a poet also: and he began remembering the close of Erigena's *De Divisione Naturae*, his prayer for the coming of the Light that will bring to darkness the false light of the philosophers, and will lighten the darkness of those that know. The memory had carried him into a soundless place, and how long he had been deaf he did not know, till beside him he heard Heloise catch her breath.

BRITTANY

> "A land there is, a little lap of earth,
>   Near neighbor to the dawn and the south wind,
>   The first to feel the sweet new-risen sun,
>   Nor hurt at all by his primaeval fire.
>   It knoweth but the clemency of heaven,
>   And in one lap holds the delights of earth.
>   Amid those happy woods a river flows
>   That winds and turns again upon itself,
>   Chiding the roots and warring with the pebbles,
>   Till with a murmuring of fleeting water
>   It falls into the levels of the lake.
>   Here to these water-meadows, flowering fair,
>   Came man, a while their guest: too brief a guest."

He heard Heloise give a long sigh: it had its echo in his own heart. If Bernard dreamed of man's lost Paradise, they two were grieving for their own.

The voice from the shadows halted, troubled. Bernard Sylvestris was hanging over his desk, frowning, aware of some vague trouble in the room, a trouble that had wakened his own eternal questioning.

"Too brief a guest," he repeated. His head sank on his breast. And again after a long silence, "Too brief a guest."

"But shall the clay say to him that fashioneth it, 'What makest thou?' Shall the thing framed say of him that framed it, 'He had no understanding'?

"Yea. The soul cries out upon the body: and I have heard the body cry out upon the soul, to the Creator of them both. 'Daily the soul complains of me,' it cried, 'because I conform to my own nature, and dishonor her daily. But Thou didst fashion me of earth: how can I but smell of it? Had I been cleanly fashioned of things clean, then might she blame me for my filthiness. But now, rather might she cry out on that which made me of such stuff, and yoked us in one yoke.' Aye, and I have seen the souls of the unborn, huddled by the house of Cancer the Crab, and pure in their simple essence, they shudder at the dull and blind habitations which they see prepared."

He was shuddering now. The short-sighted eyes wandered over the blur of young bewildered faces turned up to his, as though he sought some understanding. Suddenly he strung himself, as if he had met the challenge of the eyes burning in the shadow of the door.

" 'Dull and blind.' So dull? So blind? I tell you, let the spirit complain of the flesh no more. It is the prison which makes men free. I tell you, this flesh is the condition of their immortality. For in mastering it does the mortal become immortal, and humanity pass to the proud gods. Let you but look at a man's eyes! The beasts run downcast, looking at the earth, but the very face of man is witness to his majesty: alone on earth he rears his sacred head to the stars. The Gods themselves, and the sky, and the stars, hold speech with him: he is one with the council of the Fates, aye, and by that same base act of generation, he throws the gauntlet down to Atropos. He shall bring to light the dark causes of things, lost in the mirk: he shall see the windy fields of the air, he shall see the dark silence of the dead. His is the height of heaven, and the breadth of the earth, and the depth of the sea, and he shall know the changing face of things and why they change. He shall subdue the earth and rule upon it, the first of things created, their king and their high priest."

Again he stopped, his eyes holding those other unseen eyes, his spirit grappling with one mightier and more tormented than his. He was crouching forward now, his hands gripping the outer edge of the desk.

"But the stains: but love, *tyrannus amor*, the tyrant of our flesh: but the whole ineradicable evil of the ancient wood? So be it. Earth to earth: but be thou heaven's familiar, and let your eyes depart not from those high places. For when this house of thine falls in ruin about thee, they shall abide thy coming, familiar roofs of home. No unknown stranger shalt thou climb there, where waits thee the place and the banner of thy star."

He swayed a moment, then dropped on his seat, his arms along the desk in front of him, his eyes closed. Heloise felt Abelard's hand upon her shoulder: she rose and followed him into the sudden light. In silence they went back to the inn: and still in silence, they took the north road to Paris.

BOOK III

PARIS

July–October 1118

CHAPTER I

IT is our custom in our daily speech," wrote Abelard, "to speak of things as they appear to our bodily senses, rather than as they are in actual fact. So, judging by the sight of our eyes, we say it is a starry sky, or not, or that the sun is hot, or has no heat at all, or that the moon is shining more, or less, or even not at all, when these things, however variable they show to us, are ever in one stay. Is it any wonder, then, that some things have been stated by the Fathers, rather from opinion than from truth? Moreover, many a controversy would find a swift solution if we could be on our guard against the same word used in different senses by different authors."

The wheels drove heavily. He set down his pen and yawned. The first discovery of argument in one's own mind had always a glory about it: one could recapture something of it, watching it strike fire from the right audience: but this arguing at two removes, with a goose quill instead of the human voice, was a dry business. The preface to the *Sic et Non* must be written: it must lay down the principles for all judicious reading, whether of Holy Writ or of the Fathers: yet when he wrote, he rattled dry peas in the bladder that was his brain. It was a sullen day: there was no sun shining, and the gutters stank most vilely. He had spent most of it indoors, this Octave of St. Peter and St. Paul. He had gone to Mass that morning, in the hope that he might see Heloise, but she was not there, nor Fulbert. The Schools were empty, for the men had gone a week ago, on the 29th of June, and there was nothing to take him out.

He yawned again and came back to his manuscript, turning the pages idly. Whether Adam was created inside Paradise or out: whether Eve alone was seduced or Adam also: whether James, brother of Our Lord, was first Bishop of Jerusalem or not: whether one already baptized may be baptized again or not: whether sin was remitted in the Baptism of John or not. He scowled as he read. He knew that these had served his purpose well enough, that they proved the contradictory authority of the Fathers: he knew too that he had dealt with weightier things: but none of them, on this perverse day, would meet his eye. Here were pages on virginity, whether it be prescribed or not: whether any human copulation can be without sin: whether the married priest is to be rejected by his parishioners or not. Undoubtedly he was being happily guided in his *sortes.* "*Whether it is ever lawful for a man to marry her with whom he hath committed fornication.*" It caught him fair between the eyes. Well, what had they to say about it? He settled down to read sardonically. St. Ambrose: for any Christian to enter upon marriage with her whom he hath stained with unlawful defilement, was even as the sin of incest. Augustine, on the other hand, that legitimate marriage with good intent may well follow an illicit union, and that true marriage may follow even adultery, if the husband of the first marriage be dead. Gregory the Great, as grim as Ambrose. Council of Châlons, against. Council of Aix-la-Chapelle, against. Ivo of Chartres: that on the whole the

[164]

Fathers, concerned for the honor of marriage, denounce
it: but others, regarding the weakness and folly of their
fellows with an instinct of compassion, would fain tem-
per the rigor of the canon. *And between their opinions
seems to me just such a distance as lies between justice
and mercy.* Abelard thrust the manuscript from him and
was on his feet, snarling in sudden ungovernable fury.
Regarding the weakness and folly of their fellows . . .
between justice and mercy. . . . Let them keep their
mercy till they were asked for it. Let them turn their
backs like good old bilious Gregory and walk off holding
their noses as from the sin of incest. Anything was more
tolerable than this insufferable patronage of the saints.

"Neither do I condemn thee: go and sin no more." He
stopped his trampling up and down the room. He did
not know where the words had come from; he had been
in no humor to call them to his mind, and suddenly they
were in him, like a memory in the blood. His rage
dropped from him, though a pulse was still beating in his
cheek. He sat down, utterly exhausted, and dropped his
head on his hands. "And because He would not condemn
me," he thought, "I could lay my head in the dust."

He sat there, thinking not at all, breathing slowly.
The anger that had swept through him was like a heather
fire: for a while it had left no life in him. The bell began
ringing for Compline, and in a little while he heard, far
off and faint, the chant from the choir. It brought to him
the memory, not of the evening office, but of that morning's Mass for the octave of St. Peter and St. Paul, and
the gradual. Was there any so beautiful in all the circuit
of the year? *"The souls of the just are in the hand of*

God, and the torment of malice shall not touch them: In the sight of the unwise they seemed to die, but they are in peace."

He sat still, the remembered chant stealing like a river through the chambers of his brain. *The torment of malice:* there was strange wisdom in the liturgy that could dare to bring that hissing serpent of a word into its requiem, secure that it could not shake its peace. *The souls of the just are in the hand of God.* He got to his feet, with a quick sigh. He was far from that yet.

Standing there, saddened as he was, a sudden wave of tenderness swept over him for Heloise. He could do so little for her, body or soul. Had he done right to bring her from Denise and her kind fostering, and her little son, and Hugh the Stranger, and all that gentle country-side, to these rank gutters and that dark house? *The torment of malice*—he put it from him quickly. There was no hint of that. She had assured him, over and over, that Fulbert was kind with her, even tender, sometimes. She had looked white and cold, almost like a dead thing, at their secret marriage in St. Aignan's, but he and she had both spent the night in vigil in the church, and it was no wonder if she seemed ill and strained at dawn. As for Fulbert, he was another man. Every day seemed to fill out the little figure to its old comfortable roundness, the grease stains were gone from his cassock, and he crossed the Parvis with his old jaunty step, nodding a little, like the more important of the pigeons. To Abelard himself he was even effusive. Once only, when he brought Heloise for the first time into the old man's presence, had he seen any trace of the old rancor. At first Fulbert had had eyes only for her. He had stood, holding her in his arms,

[166]

shaking, half crying, his head buried on her shoulder. Then when he righted himself and turned to greet Abelard, there had been—or had Abelard imagined it?—the merest suggestion of a flicker in his eye, the flash of an adder into the long grass. Even if it were, thought Abelard, it would have been natural enough. And since then he had been complaisance itself.

Too complaisant. Abelard scowled at divers memories. Could the man not behave like her guardian and her uncle, instead of fawning on him like a gratified father-in-law, or worse still, leering like a pimp? Whatever ailed him, Abelard felt guiltier now in his rare visits to Heloise, than when he had been at his wit's end to contrive a meeting with her. And Heloise too seemed sometimes subdued. They laughed less, he thought sadly, yet from no weariness. Their passion was no less, but it had taken to itself a quality of tenderness that made it more poignant, less easily slaked: sometimes as she clung to him, he could feel her tears salt on his lips and could not question them, for they stung in his own eyes.

Well, he would go and see her. It was five days since he had been to the house, though he had written to her every day, and she to him. Fulbert had not been at Mass: it would be something if a touch of fever, or bile, had him in bed. Cheered even at the ghost of the possibility, he took his hood and went down the well of the stairs, and out into the dead air of the July dusk. At Le Palais they would have nearly finished cutting the hay. He had smelt new-mown hay from the fields across the river, yesterday, but there was no wind to bring it tonight, or to carry off the smell that hung about the tanneries. That seemed able to cross the river at any time. Among the cobblestones at his feet a fish's eye from its decapitated head looked up at him with a kind of white malevolence. Of such, he said to himself, are the evening primroses of Paris.

He had to stand for a while on the doorstep, after knocking. The door was never open now: that was one change from the old days of unsuspecting intimacy that had persisted, even in the new understanding, and it never failed to irk him. For unless Heloise was watching for him, it meant that he must see Grizzel, and for Grizzel, reason with himself as he might that she was only an ancient bristled sow, he had a repugnance that was more than physical. He was superstitious about meeting her. It could spoil his eagerness, as the ugly chatter of a single magpie could jar into a spring day. She had never been more than civil with him: his first coming had made more work in the house, and only his careless lavishness had kept her spite from overflowing her greed. Moreover, of late it had gone against the grain with him to give her money: it seemed to him that he was placating a bawd. He gave it to Heloise for her, instead, bidding her not say it was from him.

Had she guessed it was he at the door? The minutes seemed interminable. He was about to knock again, when he heard her grunting approach. She was watching him through the lattice of the grille, he knew, but he deliberately kept his back turned. At last he heard the bolts drawn, and the door creaked open. She looked up at him silently. More than ever the evil eye tonight, he thought. As a rule he asked for her master, but some obstinacy made him change his mind.

"Is your mistress within?"

Her lips curled back like an old bitch's snarl. "Aye, *your* mistress is," said she, then suddenly cringed. He had not struck her, but the eyes had a glance like a levin bolt and her knees gave under her.

"It was a slip o' the tongue," she mumbled, retreating against the wall. "She's in her room, sir. Not with the master. You'd better not go near the master," she cried after him, with a sudden return of the snarl.

Abelard stopped on his way to the stairs.

"Is your master ill?"

"Aye." She looked at him, powerless and malevolent. "God blast the pair of ye, that brought him to it," she said, very slowly. There was a sincerity in it that in some curious way robbed it of any offense. Abelard turned on his heel and went on up the familiar stairs, past Fulbert's room, the door closed, and on to the great room that had been his. As he climbed the next flight, and the step gave under him with its remembered groan, he heard her door open. He could almost feel the strained expectancy with which she would be listening.

"It is I, beloved," he said, very low.

She said nothing, but he heard her take her breath. She had gone back into the room, and as he came through the door she closed it behind him and caught him. Neither of them spoke. That some cruel thing ailed her, he knew, without a word from her: knew too that all she wanted for the moment was the silent holding of his arms.

In a little while she sighed and held him away from her. "Now nothing matters," she said, with a ghost of a laugh in her voice. "I have seen you again."

She drew him over to the settle and sat down, still holding him away from her. She was very white and panting

a little. In spite of the closeness of the night, she had a
wrap muffled about her throat.

"Child," he said, forgetful of Grizzel's news, "you are
not ill? Have these stinking gutters caught you in the
throat?"

"No, no. At least," she hesitated, "it is a little sore. But
nothing that matters. I have wrapped it up. Nothing
matters, now that I have seen you."

He looked at her, thoroughly uneasy.

"Is it swollen?"

She shook her head. "It is nothing. It will be well again
in the morning. No—" She drew the scarf closer round
it and moved away from his outstretched hand. "Please,
Peter. At least, not just now. Let me talk to you a little
first."

She was more like herself now, and he thought it best
to humor her.

"I was vexed," she went on, "that I did not hear you,
to let you in. Was it Grizzel?"

"It was," he said grimly. "And in a good mood too.
But tell me," he suddenly remembered the news of Fulbert, "she said your uncle was ill?"

Heloise nodded. "I think," she said quietly, "he has
had another stroke. Simon Trivet came and bled him.
He is sleeping now."

Abelard was dumb for a moment. The memory of the
first stroke, in this very room, was upon him. What had
brought the second? He could hardly bear to question
her, yet she was looking at him as if she would gladly
speak, and could not bring herself to it.

"Were you with him? Was he in his own house?"

She nodded. "It was before Vespers. Geoffrey of Chartres was here. And," her voice changed, "Alberic of Rheims."

Abelard uttered a stifled exclamation. "Together? Did they come together?"

"No. Geoffrey came first, with a message from Gilles. You know the book of Ivo's letters that I have been copying for Gilles. Geoffrey was anxious to see it, because of some trouble he is having with the Count of Chartres. Gilles says he will be a great bishop, Peter."

"Geoffrey? It is as wise a brain as there is in France." He saw that she was eager to speak of indifferent things, and went on talking of Geoffrey and his brother Hugh, the Seigneur de Lèves. He would be a better successor to Ivo than either Bernard or his brother Thierry, he said, for Bernard cared too much for Virgil, and Thierry for mathematics, to have the charge of a great diocese, above all with a ruffian like Count Thibault to keep in his place. Besides, the De Lèves were as good blood as the Counts of Chartres, and that was always a help. "Had you much talk with him?"

Heloise shook her head. "He had hardly told my uncle his errand when Alberic came in. I had never seen him before. Very fat, and small eyes peeping. He said to my uncle that he had long had a great desire to see his relic, you know, that bit of the spine of St. Evroul, and my uncle was all flattered and happy and took him to his oratory. I do not believe he came for that, I think it was only to spy. And when they came back, Alberic began talking to Geoffrey, praising the schools at Chartres and making little of his own at Rheims. I do not know why it is so much worse for a fat man to fawn than a thin one.

But Geoffrey only laughed, and said that Paris had over-topped them all, and that Chartres was become no better than a grammar school for it."

Abelard smiled grimly. "That would please Alberic."

"All the time he was watching me sideways. And then he looked down his nose and said that he had understood it was under a cloud of late, and that Master Peter Abelard was said to be beginning to repeat himself."

"Well? Had Geoffrey anything to say to that?"

The light leapt in Heloise's eyes. "He laughed, you know that light amused laugh of his. 'Don't listen to the cockroaches, Alberic,' said he. 'Do you know that I had a deal more consequence in Rome as friend to Peter Abelard than as Bishop-elect of Chartres? They call him the Socrates of Gaul.'"

Abelard was crimson with pleasure. "Geoffrey always was a good fighter," he said. "They used to say he was better at attack than defense, for by the time he had begun the first, there was no need for the second."

"There wasn't, here." Her eyes were shining. Then they clouded. She looked down at her hands.

"Well, child?" said Abelard gently. "Did it annoy your uncle to hear me praised?"

"No, oh, no," she cried. "I wish it had." She was scarlet with mortification. "I could not look at him. He sat, looking from one to the other, rubbing his hands and beaming and making little noises, and when Geoffrey had finished he began about its being very gratifying for him. Geoffrey tried to interrupt (I think he felt that something was wrong, without divining what it was), and said that as a canon of Notre Dame he must be proud to own you, but my uncle could not be stopped. He said

[172]

that he had more intimate cause than that to be proud of you, for he had always regarded this child here—and he pointed to me—as a daughter, and to know her married to so great a man—" She stopped. She could go no further.

Abelard's hand tightened on hers. It was for her reassurance, for he himself felt nothing. It had come, then. Well, what of it?

"Well, child?" he asked, so tranquilly that she stole a glance at him and took courage.

"Geoffrey had got to his feet and was saying something very loud about having to sup with Gilles, and Alberic coming too. But Alberic sat leaning forward, with his eyes darting out of his head. 'Married?' said he. 'I do indeed congratulate you on your—son-in-law,' and then he turned to me, 'and you,' said he, 'on your—Socrates.'" She paused again.

"My uncle stood there, babbling and smiling. And I said, 'I am afraid, Master Alberic, that with my uncle the wish has begotten the thought. It is his delusion that I am married to Master Peter, but it is not true.' My uncle stood staring at me. I think he hardly took in what I was saying. They all stared. And then Alberic thrust his face nearer mine and said in that pasty voice of his:

"'You are not then his wife?'"

Abelard had risen to his feet. "And you said?"

She had risen, too, confronting him, and smiling. "I said I was your mistress."

Abelard drew a sharp breath. Her courage slashed him like a sword. He stood for a moment gazing at her, his pride in her overtopping even his wonder. Then he went on one knee before her, and kissed her hand.

"Beloved, it was magnificent. But—" he rose to his feet, in sudden comprehension, "your uncle—?"

She turned away. "My uncle—" She stopped. "Ah, Peter, you can imagine it. He was shrieking and then . . . and then he fell." She sat down, as if her story was finished and there was no more to say.

Abelard was looking down at her, mentally filling in the gaps.

"Did he touch you?"

"He— Ah, what does it matter? I told you he was mad."

Abelard stooped and unwound the scarf from her throat. She did not struggle. He stood for a while looking at it.

"So he clawed you. Like a wild beast."

He dropped on his knees beside her, his head on her lap. He had brought her to this, his darling to the power of the dog.

"Beloved, it was only for a moment. They both pulled him away. He was tearing at them, too. And then suddenly he fell, in a fit. Geoffrey stayed and helped to get him to bed. And Alberic went for Simon Trivet, to bleed him. Grizzel is minding him. It is better for him not to see me yet."

Abelard got up and moved over to the window. "He is not ever going to see you again," he said briefly. "Heloise, for God's sake do not try to spare me. How long have you been in dread?"

"Do you remember the night we came? It was the look in his eyes when he turned to you. A little red speck, like on a viper's back."

"I saw it," said Abelard. "I hoped you had not."

[174]

"I was afraid for you, after that, every time you came to the house. It was one reason why I would never have you eat or drink in the house, unless I had seen to it myself, even brought up the wine from the cellar."

"But for yourself? Was he harsh with you?"

She shook her head. Then suddenly she dropped her head on her hands and began crying quietly. He came over to her then and held her. She thrust her head into the hollow of his arm.

"It was the nights," she said. "I used to waken in the dark, and know that he was standing at the foot of the bed. He would stand there, stooping forward, peering at me. And then after a long while he would go away. I couldn't bolt the door, for he had the bolt taken away after that night he found us together. I used to lie and watch it, till it began opening."

He could say nothing. His self-reproach was too bitter. She soon was quiet, lying in his arms. In a little while she touched his cheek.

"Now that I have told you," she said, "I think I shall never be afraid again."

He disengaged her then, and set her down beside him, his arm still about her shoulder.

"Listen, beloved. I shall stay with you tonight, and tomorrow you and I will ride back to Brittany."

She shook her head.

"I knew you would say that," she said, "and I have been thinking, as soon as I came up here by myself, what I must do. I knew you would not let me stay here. I do not think I could. But if we go to Brittany, it will be confirmation of everything my uncle has said. As it is, I think it was well they saw him in his madness. They will believe more easily, even Alberic, that what I said is true, that it is his delusion. And so I made up my mind that I would go, for a while anyhow, back to Argenteuil. I shall tell Reverend Mother everything. She would know it, anyhow. She is like Gilles, in that. And I am not afraid of her any more. It is odd how much I have been thinking of her of late. She is not a good woman. I used to think that she was even wicked. But she is strong. And she would never give away anything one told her. Besides, she is Gilles's cousin."

Abelard had risen and was leaning against the window, silent. Were they born with the wisdom of the ages, these women?

"I shall even ask her," Heloise went on, "if I may wear novice's dress. And everyone will be told that I am going to take the veil, in a year or two. It will give the lie to anything my uncle may say or do. Even if he brings witnesses of our marriage, it will not matter. For even if we were married, it would annul it if I took the veil."

She had grown very white. Abelard turned from the window to see the still face, the eyes that looked out at emptiness. He tried to come to her, but he could neither move nor speak. Grotesquely there came to him the memory of the clerk who set a ring on the finger of the statue of Venus in the market place, and found the marble image bedded between him and his young bride. She had gone on speaking, but he had ceased to take it in. At last he managed a kind of strangled croak.

"Heloise, have pity," he said.

The unseeing eyes came to life, in a flash she was beside him, clinging to him, kissing his sad eyes, his trembling mouth.

[176]

"Beloved, beloved, as if any vows could take me from you." For a while they stood, holding one another. He heard her murmur under her breath, "The gates of hell shall not prevail against us."

CHAPTER II

"Holy Silvester, intercede for her soul.
Holy Gregory, intercede for her soul.
Holy Martin, intercede for her soul.
Holy Alexis, intercede—"

HELOISE, kneeling behind the senior nuns in the infirmary, had ceased to follow the litany. Her eyes were no longer on Godric's face, that was not any more the face of the small indomitable scholar that she knew, but was a strange old woman's, carved for death. They were fixed on the hand that held the blessed candle, so tightly that the infirmarian would not take it from her, the small claw-like hand that was alone recognizable and that alone showed any life, for the eyes already gleamed white under the half-closed lids. If Heloise prayed at all, dazed with fatigue and a kind of slow resentment, it was that Godric might die quickly, escape from this long agony of intercession that beat and clamored round the solitude in which her soul had lived.

Three days ago they had given her extreme unction, and she was living still; if that could be called life which was only the fluttering of restless hands like the limed wings of a bird, hands athirst for death, struggling to push away the intolerable weight of life. Only when

Heloise held them were they still. But last night even her hands lay quiet, and the infirmarian had sent Heloise to bed. She had fallen straight into an abyss of sleep from which the waking had been sheer physical agony. For the waking had come with the nightmare wooden clatter of the tablet in the cloister, under the infirmarian's breathless hammering, so that the whole convent might come running to watch their sister die. And the nightmare had continued, the flapping of the wide shoes down the cloisters (the sisters may run, Heloise remembered sardonically, only to assist at a deathbed, or from a fire), the flying black gowns like dark birds speeding through the mirk, the grim preparations for the end, already begun when she reached the infirmary and took her place among the frightened, sleepy novices. The dark haircloth was already on the floor with the ghostly outline of the cross stretched out upon it, gray with the ashes that had been kept since Ash Wednesday for just such use as this. They were laying Godric upon it as Heloise knelt down. At the foot of the grave-cloth the Abbess knelt, holding up the crucifix for the blind eyes to see, her massive face graven into grim resolution. Her arm had wearied after a while, and the infirmarian had taken the crucifix from her and held it nearer still; but the deep husky voice, Gilles's voice, had swept unfaltering through the Creed, through the Penitential Psalms, and now was besieging the whole hierarchy of heaven to intercede with the Most High for this small wraith that was so soon to face Him.

> "Holy Magdalene, intercede for her soul.
> Holy Felicitas, intercede for her soul.
> Holy Agatha—"

Heloise wrung her hands in a more desperate intercession. And even as her soul cried out, the candle fell,
still burning, on the haircloth. A sigh breathed up from
the kneeling figures, swaying forward: a scared novice
began to sob. But the Abbess had risen, the burning
candle caught and held high, her face transfigured.

*"Exibit spiritus eius et revertitur in terram suam: in die
illa videbit Dominum creatorem suum."*

There was a momentary silence: then the strong voice
rose again, no longer interminably beseeching, but challenging heaven's gates like the trumpets of its returning
victorious host.

"Go forth, Christian and holy soul, from this world.
Go in peace, in the name of the Father Almighty, who
created thee: in the name of our Lord Jesus Christ, Son
of the living God, who died for thee: in the name of the
Holy Ghost, who was shed upon thee: in the name of
angels and archangels: in the name of principalities and
powers and all the strength of Heaven: in the name of
Cherubim and Seraphim: in the name of the whole
human race which is written in the Book of Life: in the
name of patriarchs: in the name of apostles and martyrs:
in the name of bishops and confessors: in the name of
priests and deacons and every order of the Catholic
Church: in the name of holy virgins and faithful widows.
Today in the Heavenly Jerusalem let thy place and thy
habitation be. Let St. Michael the Archangel receive
thee: prince of the army of Heaven. Let the angels come
to meet thee on thy way, and bring thee into the City.
Let Peter receive thee: he to whom the Lord gave the
keys of the Kingdom of Heaven. Go forth in peace, in

the name of the Father and of the Son and of the Holy Ghost, who shall give thee light and grant unto thee eternal life, and raise thee up in the resurrection at the last day.

"Lord Jesus Christ, thou good Shepherd, receive thy servant's soul."

There was a stir of rising, whispering, and holy ejaculation, but Heloise knelt in a trance of peace. She could hear the murmur of voices about the grave-cloth, the peremptory voice of the Abbess naming the four sisters of equal seniority with the dead, the little commotion as they lifted the light body to carry it to the stone table for the washing: then from outside the creak of the well-rope, and in a little while the heavy step of the portress, the buckets of water swaying on either side of her yoke. A little splashed over as she passed, and Heloise dipped her fingers in the pool it made on the uneven flags, and drew them across her hot forehead. Then the group closed round the dead-stone. "Imagine thyself on the dead-stone," the rule for meditation had said, "figure to thyself this living body of thine turned this way and that, now on thy face, now on thy back,—thy hand lifted and dropped again." She thought of Godric, small and proud, humbled now in the indignity of death, and for the first time tears stung in her eyes. Then, as if in rebuke, the Abbess's voice, harsh with fatigue but still indomitable:

"*Almighty and everlasting God, who didst deign to breathe into this human body a soul fashioned in Thy likeness . . .*" and she slipped sideways on the stone floor, her head fallen on her kind neighbor's shoulder.

It was noon when she wakened, alone in the dorter, marvelously refreshed and very hungry. She had a dim memory of stumbling, half-carried, up the stairs, and lurching down on her bed; but it might have been a week ago, so deep was the gulf of sleep into which she had fallen and from which she now climbed. By the movement of feet in the refectory and the chanting of the grace, she guessed that dinner must have begun, if indeed it were not the grace for the ending; and waiting only to splash water on her face, she hurried down the stairs, and stood with bent head before the Abbess's table, in silent apology for her lateness. The Abbess looked at her over the chicken-bone she was tearing and nodded: a gross woman, thought Heloise, but a mountain.

The novices were coming backwards and forwards from the kitchen, with the platters and bowls: they would not sit down till the sisters had eaten. Heloise joined them, feeling more ravenous for the good vapor that rose from the steaming bowls of soup. At the lectern a novice was reading the life of St. Pelagia, harlot of Antioch, her voice dragging and running, and sometimes yawning with fatigue, but no one paid any heed. Weary and over-watched as they were, they sat in pleasant lassitude, content to be alive and in a warm September, forgetting while they might that dread awakening at dawn, and the vigils that still lay before them. Above the Abbess's table a stiff Virgin dandled her child. Beneath her, four places were empty: the sisters would be watching in chapel, where the broken shell that had been Godric lay.

Reverend Mother struck the table with a wooden mal-

let. When grace was sung, she stood a moment, her hand
lifted to hold their attention.

"Four of you will go to the chapel and take the place
of the sisters now keeping watch. Let the rest of you
go to the dorter and lie down on your beds, and let there
be no reading or talking, for you had little sleep last night.
Let none of you presume to rise till the bell rings for
Nones, but let you sleep while you can. It may be we
shall have less of this slovenly singing in choir, such as
this morning." She looked at them for a while, her full
lips protruding and her brows scowling. "The four for
the vigil until Nones will be Gisela, Audere, Constance—"
Her eye traveled round the submissive faces. "Heloise,
you have watched at night more than any of these, but
you have most lately slept and are wakeful enough now
by the look of you, let you be the fourth."

The four went quietly down the cloister, two by two.
At the chapel door, Heloise paused for a moment, to look
out through the cloister arches. The September sun, the
sun that colored the grape, seemed to press down upon
the quiet grass, brooding above the earth like a dove. But
not the Holy Ghost.

Requiem aeternam donat ei . . .

she heard the murmur of prayer as the three passed the
threshold, and quietly she turned to follow.

Et lux perpetua luceat ei.

She paused to cross herself with holy water, and passed
up to the choir.

It was always dark in the choir: that was why Godric
had stumbled and fallen, two years ago. But candles

burnt about her now, and a stoup of holy water stood at her head. Godric was more like herself: they had dressed her in her habit, and she was sound asleep. Heloise slipped to her knees at the foot of the bier, and took the service book that Gisela handed her, open at the Commendation of the Dead. *Deus immensae pietatis,* Audere began, but for a moment Heloise could not echo her, for she was blind with tears. It was not the sight of the dead. Godric had died days and days before, when the last flicker of that shining intelligence had faded out of the eyes and left them blank and staring. It was the sight of the handwriting on the vellum page, the small, perfectly balanced script, with the suspicion of the Irish character still about the r's. This was the Godric that she knew, and as she looked and stumbled through the prayer, the slow resentment that had smoldered in her during the litany of intercession burnt again. Why did they labor it so, this act of dying? Godric, intent like a small wrinkled toad over her parchment, this was the Godric that mattered, and Heloise's heart rose in a blind defiance, a *Therefore choose life.*

The *Deus immensae pietatis,* the *Diri vulneris perculsi* dragged their course. They had begun again the prayer of which she had heard the opening at the washing of the dead, but she was reading mechanically. What her eyes saw was the crabbed page of the book of Alcuin's Letters that had come from the Abbot of Corbei, the small bent figure in the bed, the bright eyes. *"Ah, but they were good days when you and I sat quiet among the bookshelves."* The hours of that forgotten September day passed before her, small and clear and far off like the illuminated border of a page of script. Two years ago,

only, for today was again the Eve of the Dedication of
St. Michael the Archangel: but it belonged to some other
life. She saw herself in the bees' garden, in the shadow
of the boxwood hedge, and about her the white parched
grass, but the girl that she saw was a stranger. Yet that
girl reading there had thought she loved. *"I beseech you
therefore, brethren, by the mercies of God, that ye present your bodies a living sacrifice"*—she remembered how
it had shivered through her, a blasphemy intolerably
sweet. Heloise, watching, found her heart going out to
her in an aching protective compassion. If she had died
then, had gone out knowing only that crystalline brittle
world of first love, that soundless, narrow world where
two walk alone, with neither heaven nor hell, not knowing that in love there is moan or cry! Would she hold
her there, ignorant and passionate, prison her for ever
under that cloudless blue, with the colorless grass at her
feet and the river slipping by, time become eternity? For
if she chose, it seemed to her, she could call back yesterday.

Uneasily aware of some strangeness beside her, Gisela
turned to look. Heloise was kneeling, her head unbowed,
her back taut as a bowstring, every tinge of color gone
from her cheeks and lips, but her eyes fixed, shining, on
something very far off. If it was a trance, she must not be
touched: it might be, thought Gisela, that she saw some
holy thing, St. Michael the Archangel, come to show
Godric the way: for was it not the Eve of his Feast? But
with it all, she was afraid. Still praying, she leaned forward once more to asperge the dead, and the words of
the prayer came more urgently, breaking into Heloise's
consciousness as human voices do when the surge of the

sea is still in the ears of the swimmer. "*Drive back, we beseech thee, O Lord, the princes and powers of darkness: receive, O Lord, thy creatures, not fashioned by any strange god, but by thee, that art alone the living and the true, for there is none beside thee, O God. . . . Remember not their ancient transgressions, nor the drunkenness that was wrought in them by the madness of evil desire: yea, they have sinned, but they have not denied thee.*" The color had come back to Heloise's face: her voice was audible again, very low but with an under-note of passion. Gisela wondered at it. She could not know that the prayer was offered not for Godric but for another.

The *Commendatio Mortis* had come to its end, and the watchers were at the third of the Penitential Psalms, when the chapel door came softly open, and the nave behind them was suddenly bright. The door swung to again, and one of the sisters, pausing only to cross herself with holy water, came uncertainly up the aisle. Her face had the glazed look of one just roused from sleep, and she yawned shamefacedly, holding her long sleeve across her mouth. She took the asperge, sprinkled the dead, and knelt down beside Heloise.

"Reverend Mother," she whispered, "bids you wait for her in the refectory. She sent for me to take your place till Nones."

Heloise, perplexed but still half dreaming, rose silently to her feet, stooped above Godric, and went down the nave. Again the door opened, letting in a great glare of warmth and brightness. It closed behind her, and she stood, dazzled, in another world.

It was close on two o'clock, and in all that sunny place

there was no stir. The very pigeons were asleep on the dorter roof. The silence seemed more mysterious in the bright undertide, with only the busy sun afoot, high in the sky, and breathing close to her so many souls asleep, wrapt from him and from all knowledge of the day. She came out from the cloister and stood a moment, leaning with her arms outstretched against the sunbaked wall, letting its warmth steal through her body that was chilled and cramped with long kneeling in the dark. And as suddenly as she had stepped from dark to light, so did she seem to have stepped from death to life. For a moment there in the candle-light it had seemed to her that the years between were blotted out. Now, it seemed, this moment of still intensity of heat and light held for her the quintessence of those years. Beside her, trellised on the wall, almost on a level with her head, there hung a great dark rose; she turned and looked into its strange heart, smiling a half-defiant recognition. Reaching up her hand, she caught it and dragged it from the wall, exulting in the battle with its strong green stem and the great thorns it had. She had it now, though it had torn her hand. *Wherefore choose life.*

With a start, she remembered her errand, and bowing her head came back under the arch, to pass down the cloister to the refectory. What had happened to raise Reverend Mother out of her bed in the middle of the afternoon, and why, if she had a charge to give her, had she not bidden Heloise to come to her in her own lodging? It was most likely a mistake of poor Emmelot's, sleepy as she was: she would look first in the refectory and then go to Reverend Mother's room, saying nothing of the blunder. O God, this spider's web of woman's life,

with its small panic fears and caution and obsequiousness!
She crushed the rose to her mouth, stifling against it a
little weary moan. Suddenly, with no warning, a fit of
tearless sobbing shook her; she stood for a moment, her
face working, her shoulders shaking with a soundless crying. Only for a moment. Could she not do this for him,
who was the heart of her body, the intelligible meaning
of her life; forgo for a little while his human nearness,
that she might keep his fame? Was it not enough that
he desired her with no less longing than her own? Was
there any so blessed among women? Her head high and
her eyes alight, she came down the cloister as though
blown before a wind. Silently she closed the great door
into the refectory, and stood gazing down its dim vaulted
length. It was as she had thought. There was no one there.
And then she saw him.

He was standing in the embrasure of a window, his
eyes fixed on the further door. So intent he was, and so
silently had she come, that his ear had caught no sound;
but the strained expectation of his attitude, the defense-
less longing on his face, caught unawares, brought a sob
to her throat. He turned and saw heaven opened, as
might a damned soul.

"Beloved," he began, when at last they spoke; "I
thought—" he shuddered and could hardly get it out—"I
thought for a while it was you that was dead."
She looked up, startled.
"I had ridden out to dine with Abbot Adam, at St.
Denis. And at dinner word came from the kitchen—some
beggarman that was here for broken meats this morning—
that there was someone dead at Argenteuil. They did not

know who it might be. But I was sure. I know, I know"
—for her eyes were chiding him—"but all last night I was
dreaming of you. No, not of you, for I could not find
you, but I was wandering all night on strange roads looking for you, standing in strange houses watching for you
to come to me. And even here—O beloved, if you knew
how I watched that door."

"But did they not tell you here?"

He nodded. "I got away from St. Denis as soon as I
decently could. And rode here. I was nearly mad when
I got here. But," he laughed a little, "your portress is a
friendly soul. Before I had time to say a word, she was
telling me before I was well off my horse how long it
took poor Godric (God rest her) to die. Dear heart, forgive me. But I would have seen every one of them dead
of the plague and thanked God, if you would but come
through that door."

She leaned against him, her head against his breast.
Suddenly she started up.

"But Reverend Mother—" Then she put down her head
again, laughing softly. "So this is what she meant when
she sent word that I was to wait for her in the refectory."

"I asked for her. I knew I must. And the portress was
very loath to disturb her, I could see, but I persuaded her.
And, God bless her, she sent word that she would see me
after Nones, but that meantime I might wait in the refectory. I guessed what she meant."

"Then no one knows you are here but Reverend
Mother and the portress?"

Abelard nodded. He got up restlessly and walked over
to the window that looked out on the cloister garden.
"Heloise, why is it so still?"

[188]

"It is always quiet between dinner and Nones. But today I think they are dead with sleep, for last night they were all roused to see Godric die."

"Are they all asleep?"

"All but the four that are keeping vigil in the chapel."

He turned from the window and looked about him, frowning at the great spaces of the hall. His eye went to the Abbess's table, and above it to the niche where the Virgin sat holding her child, Mother and Son gazing out from the wall with the same blank eyes.

"Heloise, is there nowhere we can speak but this?"

She shook her head. "One of the novices is to be received tomorrow, and her people are come already to the guest house. That is why Reverend Mother sent you here."

"Anyhow, I'd rather be in the open. If no one is about," he scowled at having to say it, "could you not take me to that bees' garden you told me of, beside the river?"

She looked troubled. "It is beyond the graveyard. And," she flushed, "the sexton from St. Julien is digging Godric's grave."

He uttered an impatient sound, and began pacing up and down the hall. Heloise watched him unhappily.

"Beloved, we have such a little while. Will you not come and sit by me, so that at least I can feel you beside me?"

He turned at the Abbess's table, and looked at her almost harshly.

"I can't. You do not know. I dare not be near you." And with that he began again his caged-beast pacing, talking now, jerkily at first, but gradually with a kind of resolute absorption: of the crowd of new students,

[189]

of an idea that he had for a book on the Trinity, and how Gilles shook his head over it, imploring him to stick to his Universals in bulk, and not confine himself to three. There's safety in numbers, said Gilles. Fulbert? Fulbert was well again, very much as when she was with him. This time there had been no relapse to the old shrunken misery.

"I sometimes think," he went on, "that he has accepted it, that you are going to take the veil, and finds a kind of appeasement in it. There is more life in the old man than I have seen for a long time."

Her face shadowed. "I do not like it. Abelard, he is dangerous, you do not know how dangerous. Sometimes I wake at night and see him—see him creeping up your stair."

Abelard shook his head at her. "Child, ever since you came here, the door at the stair foot is barred at night. Gilles made me see to that. And I sleep now in the inner room, and Guibert in the great room, with his pallet across the door."

"Guibert! But when is he ever in at night?"

Abelard halted at the window, his face cloudy, though he was wryly smiling. "Poor Guibert," he said. "We're a sorry pair, Heloise. There's little for him in the Rue des Marmousets now. Bele Alys has been weary of him this long time. It was a marvel to me she endured him as long as she did, but she is a good-natured soul, and now and then he had his turn, between lovers maybe, or if he had a new song for her. But she just cannot abide him any longer. She spat at him in the street, God help him. And then—I think to get rid of him—she told him he could have her for a night if he brought her a hundred

gold besants, and until he did that he wasn't to come in
her sight, or the bargain was off. I told him she was mocking him: for she might as well ask him for Anjou and
Maine. But he will not believe it. And the creature, he
sits there at night, copying some old lecture notes I gave
him; he sells them to the new students. There's a little
bag he keeps under his mattress. And it is a bold man
would come up those stairs at night, for with that pitiful
purse of his, he is like a cat with her kittens." He had
leant his arm against the window, and his head upon it.
"God, but it's quiet. It's like the stillness before the Last
Day." He was silent for a little while.

"Many a time I've laughed at him, Heloise, but he is
no laughing matter now.

Dira vi amoris teror.

And he'll be the ruin of me yet," he went on ruefully,
"for every sou I have about me when I come in goes into
that pitiful bag. It's something to see one human creature
happy, if only for the length of time it takes to open the
little bag and chink the coin down. And there's times
I'm fool enough to think that our two fates depend on it.
That some day—some day he and I will have our hearts'
desire."

His voice shook on the last words. With a little cry
she was beside him, turning him towards her, her hands
on his shoulders. He shivered as she touched him, then
stood rigid looking down at her. And something in the
strained whiteness of her face, the intolerable gray draperies that muffled her, broke his last defense, roused in
him the panic terror that had driven him that night in

[191]

Holy Week. He stooped and lifted her off her feet, to carry her to the dais.

"Abelard—Abelard—not here."

He was muttering, half sobbing, words that she could not hear, and her own cry was stifled. Above them the Mother of God sat dandling her child, gazing blankly from the wall. Even as her head fell back, she saw those unseeing eyes: then her own, beneath his kisses, were blind.

CHAPTER III

> "Down from the branches fall the leaves,
> A wanness comes on all the trees,
> The summer's done.
> And into his last house—"

"Have some wit, man," said Thibault crossly. "Who wants a song with a drip at the nose like that, and it hardly October?"

"Let him finish, Thibault," said Foulques Mascaron of Toulouse. "It's a good tune. Is that Master Peter's, Guibert?"

"Aye. He made it last week." Guibert looked about him a little anxiously. His master had given him leave for the day and had himself ridden out of Paris half an hour ago; but he was incalculable these times. However, the crowd was growing. He had chosen a good pitch above the river steps at the Port St. Landry, for he caught the people coming in from the country for the Michaelmas fair, as well as the scholars.

PARIS

"Get on with it, then," said Thibault, resigned. He had
a cup and ball, and was practicing a turn of the wrist that
did wonders.

> "The swollen river rushes on
> Past meadows whence the green has gone.
> The golden sun
> Has fled our world. Snow falls by day,
> The nights are dumb."

Thibault sat down on the parapet, his shoulders
hunched to his ears and his hands tucked into his sleeves.
All his friends, except the thin Foulques, eyed him delightedly.

> "About me all the world is stark
> But I am burning. In my heart
> There is a fire,
> A living flame in me, the maid
> Of my desire."

"Aha!" said Thibault, rubbing his hands.

> "Her kisses, fuel of my fire,
> Her tender touches, flaming higher,
> The light of light
> Dwells in her eyes. Eternity
> Is in her sight."

"Ah, for God's sake!" said Thibault, genuinely dis-
appointed. "Why didn't you tell us it was an *Ave?* Bring
us a warming-pan, somebody. Here, Guibert, stop that
and give us the *Abbot of Angers.*"

Indifferently Guibert tightened a string and obeyed.

> "Once there was an   Abbot of Angers,
> And the name of   the first man did he bear,
> And they say he   had a mighty thirst,
> Even beyond the   townsmen of Angers."

By the second line Thibault had joined in, and by the
time they had reached the chorus

> "Ho and ho and ho and ho,
> Glory be to Bacchus!"

they were all shouting, even Foulques, and Guibert saved
his voice and contented himself with strumming the ac-
companiment.

"That's better," said Thibault. "Now give us the one
about Margot, you know,

> "Fat, fat
> Was Margot's cat—"

"For God's sake yourself," said Foulques, "I've heard
you at nothing else, out of bed and in, for the last week.
God knows I'd as soon hear the animal itself. See here,
Guibert," he put down a couple of sous, "can you sing
'Pus vezem de novelh fleurir'?"

"Yah!" said Thibault. "Provence. Nobody in Provence
has got any guts." The ball was coming down as he spoke.
Foulques's hand swept up to meet it, seemed only to flick
it with a fingernail, and it crashed with a resounding
smack on Thibault's head. It would have felled any
other man, but on Thibault it was as though a fly had
settled. All the same, he caught his friend's head between
his knees and chastised him soundly.

"That'll teach you," said he. He backed to his old seat
on the parapet, Foulques's head still gripped in a vise.

[194]

"No, Foulques, you don't get up. You can listen nicely the way you are. Sing, Guibert, sing him what he wants."

Guibert's sunken, unchanging eyes looked out indifferently above his flute. He played a bar or two, softly trying out the tune, put down the flute, and reached for his guitar.

"Now for I see the fields in flower,
The orchards green and clear the rills and fountains,
Soft airs and wind,
It seems but just that every man should find—"

"Ow!" yelled Thibault, leaping suddenly into the air.

—"His share of joy."

There was a roar of laughter from the crowd. Foulques was on his feet, disheveled but happily smiling, his stylus in his hand.

"Call it quits, Thibault," said he. "That came very apt, Guibert. Go on."

"And if I have less joy than other men,
It is because I wish what cannot be.
This fate was given to me,
Never of what I loved to have delight.
So was it and so shall it be again,
That at the height
Of ecstasy, my heart still said to me
'All this is vain.' "

The crowd of young men were silent, overshadowed for a moment by an experience beyond them. Thibault was the first to recover.

"Just what I was saying," said he. "Nobody in Provence has got any guts."

Even Foulques laughed at that, gratefully. Guibert, meantime, was wiping his flute.

"Guibert," said Thibault suddenly, "do you ever laugh at anything? Look at him. Did ever you see as sad eyes out of a monkey's head?"

"It was in the Rue des Marmousets he got them," said an ill-conditioned youngster, anxious to be witty.

Guibert leapt to his feet, taut and quivering like a tormented cat.

"Don't heed him, Guibert," said Thibault. "An oaf like that. But see here, it's time we paid the piper." He took up Guibert's guitar and went the rounds with it, twisting the ears of the niggardly, and demanding from the last speaker a double contribution, under penalties hissed in his ear but efficacious. He brought it back, with mock solemnity. Guibert's eyes lit like lamps. There was silver among the copper, more than he had seen for days.

"Make the most of it, Guibert," said Thibault warningly. "There'll be less of this by the end of term, I can tell you. But by that time you can be writing letters home for us, on commission. Foulques here has got the loan of one about starving in hospital would draw money from an archdeacon. And, by the same token, there's old Fulbert stepping out of his own side door. What's bitten him, to be out so spry and early? Coming this way, too. I'll wager he has heard you singing, Guibert, and is out to ask for a song."

Guibert seized his guitar and made to be off down the Rue de l'Enfer, but Thibault seized his arm.

"Stand your ground, man. It's Grizzel has the evil eye. Do you remember the time we caught her cat and made him throw the dice between his forepaws, and sent him

[196]

home with the bill of his debts round his neck? Foulques, what do you bet that Fulbert doesn't ask Guibert here for a song?"

"Drinks all round," said Foulques briefly.

"That Fulbert doesn't ask Guibert for a song?"

"Aye."

"Done," said Thibault, "and I'll bet you drinks all round that he does."

The little crowd waited, laughing, yet with a laughter that gradually flickered out. There was something oddly purposeful about the little figure stepping briskly along the quay, an air of curious elation. Thibault, who had made the wager from sheer inconsequence, felt suddenly uneasy as he neared them. As if a magnet drew him, he was bearing straight down upon their little group. He was rosy in the fresh wind, and smiling, but the eyes under the white eyebrows had a gleam that was not of merriment.

"Good morning, gentlemen," said he. "You have good entertainment. I heard you from my window yonder. Guibert, it is a long time since I heard you sing last, in my own house. Will you do an old man a kindness, and come back with me?"

Guibert's bewildered eyes slid away, flickering wretchedly from face to face. The group had fallen silent, but they had unconsciously withdrawn a little, leaving a clear space between the two. Thibault was making faces at him behind Fulbert's back, honest school-boy faces of dissuasion. It gave him courage to look up at last into the innocent, rosy countenance that beamed upon him.

"I was just going to the Grand Pont, your reverence,"

he said. "I'll miss the crowds else. The folk are coming to the market, you see. This was just by way of daffing and sport." It was a long time since Guibert had strung as many sentences together, but the words seemed to put up a kind of fence between him and the other.

"I had no thought but to make it worth your while," said Fulbert. He came forward and laid a coin on Guibert's guitar.

Guibert made a little sound in his throat. He looked up, dumbfounded, into Fulbert's face, but even the eyes were smiling now.

"Gold?" he whispered.

Fulbert nodded. With a flash like the monkey Thibault had likened him to, the coin was snatched up and hidden. He was on his feet and following Fulbert, walking like a man in his sleep. The old man, now that he had gained his end, looked neither to right nor left, but set off back along the quay to his own house. The young men watched without a word. Only Thibault, shaking himself awake, grasped at Guibert as he went by.

"Don't go, Guibert," he whispered urgently. "There's some hell-broth brewing."

But Guibert looked up at him, still dazed.

"It was gold," he said, and went on.

Thibault crossed himself. "For God's sake," said he, "let's go and have a drink."

"You've won your bet, Thibault," said the ill-conditioned lad who had made the joke about the Rue des Marmousets.

Thibault seized him, turned him upside down, and held his face in the gutter.

"And that's your share of the drinks," said he.

Guibert stood, barely inside the threshold of Fulbert's room. The door was open behind him. Fulbert moved briskly to the wall-press by the fire.

"It's ill singing on an empty belly," said he. "You look cold, Guibert." He poured him out a drink, and another for himself.

"Shut the door and sit down, man," he said kindly. "Here, bring your stool over to the fire, and drink in comfort." He stooped to turn the log on the hearth, and Guibert took advantage of his back being turned to make the sign of the cross above the wine. Still, the old lad was drinking it himself, and what with the outer door being on the latch, he had not so far seen Grizzel. A kitten asleep on the warm hearth awoke, yawned a preposterous, tiny yawn, pranced delicately on its paws, and made a dart at the tassels of his guitar. He lifted it on his knee, and it was friendly and dug its claws into his hose and purred and suddenly slept. He was glad to feel it there. He held up his head and drank courageously, and the wine warmed him, a gentle warmth, like the warmth of the kitten's little body on his thigh.

Fulbert, it seemed, had nothing to say to him, and that also was a relief. Maybe it was a sudden notion the old man had taken. Not so long ago he had been astray in the head, though sensible enough of late. Well, if it was madness, it had taken a good turn for him. If only Grizzel would not come in, and make a scolding-match, and maybe take the gold piece from him. He looked uneasily at the door.

"Grizzel's at the market," said Fulbert.

Guibert nodded and settled himself more comfortably

on his stool. He had finished his wine, and to show that he was diligent to earn his fee, he took his guitar and began tuning it.

"That's right," said Fulbert. "There was a song you used to sing when you were here, Guibert. Two years ago. I believe it was one of Master Peter's." Guibert stole an uneasy look at him, but there was no crack in the smooth benevolence of the face. "Something about the summer coming in, and a young wench. Do you remember it?"

Guibert looked embarrassed. "There's a many about that, please your reverence," said he. "Could you maybe mind a little more about it? Not but what I'll sing you all I know and welcome, but maybe you would weary."

Fulbert looked down at his hands. "There was one line," he said, "like *Ut mei misereatur*." His voice was thin.

Guibert flinched. If it had been any song but that. He had not dared to sing it in the streets for months, because the last time he had sung it he had broken down and they had gibed at him. But it might be easier here, in this quiet place, with the gentle old man. The old man would not laugh at him. And anyhow the first two verses were easy enough. He struck a few notes on his guitar.

"That's it," said Fulbert. He sat back in his chair, his hand over his eyes.

> "When summer on its stealing,
>   And come the gracious prime
> And Phoebus high in heaven
>   And fled the rime,

> With love of one young maiden
>> My heart hath ta'en its wound,
>> And manifold the grief that I
>>> In love have found."

Fulbert sat forward, his elbows on his knees, his hands covering his face. And for once Guibert's mind left the thought of Bele Alys and the torture of that remembered gesture that had once been for him, and then no more, and bent itself on the old man's strange trouble.

> "Ut mei misereatur,
>> Ut me recipiat,
>> Et declinetur ad me,
>>> Et ita desinat.

> "If she would once have pity
>> And take me to her side,
>> And stooping lean down o'er me,
>>> And so abide."

The room fell silent. The old man sat all huddled in his chair. Suddenly he raised his head.

"Et declinetur ad me," he cried in a strange loud voice. "Never, never, never." He leaned across to Guibert, gesticulating, his hands shaking as if in a palsy.

"He took her from me. He made her hate me, my little one, my white wood sorrel, my white doe. He smutched her, and had his dirty will of her, and now he's tired of her"—his voice rose to a scream—"and he's flung her, like foul water, on the ash-heap at Argenteuil."

Guibert sat, too terrified to speak or move.

"He'll make a nun of her," he went on. "She that was meant to be a man's darling, she that he took to wife before my own eyes, at St. Aignan, just two doors away.

He'll make a nun of her, so that he can break the marriage and be priested." His voice dropped. "I'll priest him," he said, very low. Suddenly he turned on Guibert.

"What are you gaping at, you fool? Haven't you heard it?"

Guibert shook his head. "The young mistress is at Argenteuil, sure enough," he said, placating. "But I never heard that the master had any notion of orders, beyond what he has already."

"Orders? Haven't I heard them in this very room joking him about being the Lord Pope some day? Why else should he send her to Argenteuil? Isn't she going about in her grave-clothes, all but the veil, that they'll put on her—aye, the Bishop here will put on her—in a six months? And then my holy Master Peter will come ambling up to take his vows of chastity too. Chastity." He stood up and clawed the air. "But I'll save him the trouble. Aye, I'll save him any trouble there. He'll sleep sound of nights when I've done with him."

Guibert leapt to his feet, his own fear forgotten. "Master Fulbert," said he, "may God forgive you. You would not murder him?"

"Fulbert's hands dropped. He stood stock-still for a moment, peering into Guibert's face. The demoniac light flickered out. "Man alive, what put that in your head? No, no, I wouldn't murder him. I hope he'll live long, long, long, the way I would have him. Long and chaste." He giggled. "Sit down, lad. What's your hurry?"

Guibert sat, rather because his knees gave under him, than from any wish ever to sit in this accursed presence again.

"He'll live chaste, but he won't be a priest, Guibert,"

the old man went on. "I've been reading a deal, these days. It takes a whole man to be a priest. Do you know that they couldn't make offering even of a gelded beast, Guibert?"

Guibert opened his mouth to cry out, but he could not. Deadly sickness had taken him, and it seemed to him that the chair with the old man in it was heaving up and down. With a mighty effort he thrust his sickness down, keeping his head low in his hands.

"But he'll live the holier for it. Didn't Our Lord say that some have made themselves eunuchs for the kingdom of heaven's sake? I doubt Master Peter will never do that, Guibert, but I know some will do it for him."

Guibert had but one thought, to get away, to tell the Bishop, to have this man shut up, somewhere, before his master came back that night. Was he to be waylaid even this very day? He rose again to his feet.

"I must be going, your reverence," he said steadily. "Thank you kindly for the wine. But I'll give you back your gold piece, if you don't mind, your reverence." His fingers were on it where it burnt above his heart, like her own touch, but they faltered. He saw the curve of her shoulder as she stooped over him. He had almost two pieces towards the hundred. This would make it almost three.

"You earned it fairly, man. I don't want it back," said Fulbert. The craziness had gone from his face and voice. He was talking quietly and gravely. "But I want to put you in the way of earning a deal more. Look, Guibert" —he drew a long purse suddenly from below the cushion on his chair—"how much do you think there is in that?"

"I'd say there might be fifty," said Guibert hoarsely.

"There's a hundred," said Fulbert, "and they'll be yours this night, if you choose."

Guibert opened his mouth to speak, but his throat was dry. He swallowed once or twice.

"I'll be going, your reverence," said he.

"But I have never told you what I want you to do," said Fulbert reasonably. "Listen, Guibert. I do not want you to lay a finger on him. But do you go out tonight to see Bele Alys and leave the door open as you have many a night; and give your master this that I have here"—he held up a tiny parchment packet between finger and thumb—"in his posset, to keep him sleeping till you come back again. I swear to you that you'll find him safe and well. Well enough. I mean him no harm, I tell you. I have a Jew physician trysted that will be a deal more skillful than any Christian leech. He was prisoner with the Saracens himself, you see." He giggled again.

"I'll be going, your reverence," said Guibert again. If he could but keep on saying it till he was out of the door and in the outside air. Whether it was the wine, or the dizzy sight of that gold, but the warm sweetness of her was breathing about him, his feet struggling and slipping as he remembered them once in a quicksand, when they were bathing in the Loire.

"As you please," said Fulbert tranquilly. "It is all one. But mind you, the thing will be, soon or later. There are other ways. But this secures him with least risk of hurt."

Guibert shook his head. Dizzy, he was groping for the latch of the door.

"There's no hurry," said Fulbert. He came nearer, and thrust the little packet into Guibert's hand. "Anyhow, give him this in his posset. It will only give him a good night's sleep. And if you hear an owl in the night and come down the stairs and open the door, there'll be this in my hand for you. And you need look neither this way nor that way, but go your way to the Rue des Marmousets, and no one the wiser."

Without a word, without a backward glance, Guibert stumbled through the door, and was sick in the gutter. But the packet was still in his hand.

The light was still in her window. She would open it when she heard the knocking at the door, and lean out with the candle-light behind her, as she had done a score of times, and then no more. He was knocking, but she was not looking out. Should he try hooting like an owl? He had not given Master Peter the stuff in his posset. He was guiltless of that. It was not his fault if Master Peter lay sleeping like a log with his day's riding, when the owl cried outside. He had gone in and looked at him, had even cried his name. If he had wakened then, Guibert said to himself, he would have told him. But he had not wakened. It was meant to be. He must knock louder. She must have fallen asleep with the candle still burning. There, he could hear the latch.

"Who's there?" That sleepy, husky voice that was his heaven to hear.

He stepped out from under the overhang of the house to look up at her, and dared not. The moonlight fell on his closed eyes.

"Lord ha' mercy!" she cried out. "It's a dead man."

A man's head came beside hers and a man's laugh came down to him.

"It's that poor fish Guibert," said a man's voice. "Run home, Guibert, there's a good lad."

He stood looking up at them. "Let me in," he said. "I've brought the money just as she said. Let me in."

He heard her give an impatient Tcha under her breath.

"He's clean crazed," the man said, compassionately enough. "See here, Guibert," he leaned out, broad-fronted, the candle-light gilding the bronze of his hair, "it's my turn tonight. Go home, like a good lad. To-morrow's a new day."

"Tomorrow!" Guibert screamed in sudden agony. To-morrow the world would end, but he would have had tonight. Tomorrow they would break him on the wheel, but she would have held him tonight. He stood looking up at them, trying to find words to explain it to them, but the right words would not come. He was mouthing at them, his hands clawing in the air.

Bele Alys shivered. "Mother of God," she muttered under her breath. "Wait, Roger." She slipped back into the room and came again. "Give him this—they say he's greedy for money these days—and get him to go home. It'll maybe distract him, poor soul."

Roger hung out again. "Look, Guibert," he said, holding out a bright coin. "Here's a whole silver mark for you, if you go home like a good lad, and go to bed. Catch!"

The coin tinkled in the cobbles of the street. Guibert laughed.

"Silver?" he said contemptuously. He pulled the purse from his tunic and held it up. "Look yourself. That's gold."

They were talking under their breath to each other

now. In a moment they would come down and let him in. But instead the man leaned out and began unfastening the shutters from their iron hooks and pulling them across the window.

Guibert stood frozen. "Stop!" he cried, in a voice so peremptory that Roger paused involuntarily and Alys's head appeared again above his shoulder. The poor soul was busy plucking at the strings of his purse. They watched, puzzled, and Bele Alys, bewildered and contrite, pressed for comfort on the solid shoulder above which she leaned, and put her head against his.

Guibert had his hand in the purse now. "Look!" he cried, and raising his eyes, held up his fist to show them. He saw the curve of her shoulder in the candle-light, he saw the droop of her head.

"*Et declinetur ad me*," he said, in Fulbert's voice. "Never, never, never." His voice climbed higher with every iteration. Then with a sudden shriek he flung the fistful of gold into their startled faces and, all reason gone from him, began tearing the silk purse asunder and throwing the gold pieces into the air, throwing them higher and higher, leaping with them and laughing like a crazed juggler.

"God have mercy on us," said Roger. He pulled to the shutter and stood shaking. The wild laughter and the patter of gold suddenly ceased: there was a moment's quiet. Roger looked cautiously through a crack in the shutter.

"God help him, he's on his knees trying to pick it up again."

Bele Alys looked up, her eyes brimming. "I'll go to him," said she. "I can't endure it."

Roger put his arm about her shoulder. "You'll go to no madman," said he. "He'll soon tire. Lass, is there nowhere at the back of the house we can go? They're like children, they'll cry as long as there's anyone to heed them."

She nodded, gulping, and took the candle. Even in Margot's bed, by a good chance that night empty, they heard a muffled knocking, but it did not last long. Bele Alys cried a little, but he comforted her. And when after a while the knocking ceased and a low dreary sobbing began, they did not hear it.

It was Foulques, indeed, who found it intolerable. Thibault and he were sound sleepers, and the Rue des Marmousets was accustomed to noises in the night. He had slept through most of the clatter, but the last frantic knocking had wakened him, and the low sound that followed it was more than he could bear. He kicked Thibault, and got out of bed.

"What is it?" said Thibault sleepily.

"Can't you hear it? There's somebody got hurt outside."

Thibault listened. "Sounds more like a puppy they've shut out, to me." He got up, and began pulling on his long hose.

Foulques looked out. "It's under Bele Alys's house," he said. "Can't see with the overhang. Man, it's maybe somebody knifed. There's money spilt all over the road."

Joyfully the two pulled on their breeches and were down the stairs and into the street. They saw a small figure crouching on Bele Alys's doorstep, rocking to and fro, its head in its hands.

"It's Guibert, God help him," said Thibault. "I suppose she won't let him in." He went over and touched him on the shoulder. Guibert did not look up.

"Run along home, Guibert," he said. "She'll be fast asleep by now. Better luck tomorrow."

"Tomorrow," whispered Guibert. "Tomorrow," he said again, and began shuddering.

The two boys looked at each other doubtfully. Foulques had a sudden inspiration. He stooped in turn over Guibert, and pointed to the road. "Don't cry, man," he said encouragingly. "You haven't lost it. Here's the money, spilt all over the road. We'll help you pick it up." He stooped and lifted a coin, as one encourages a child. "Look, Guibert." He held it close to the indifferent eyes. His voice changed. "Lord help us, it's gold!"

"It's gold," agreed Guibert. "He said gold."

The two exchanged glances. Then a kind of horror dawned on Thibault's face.

"This morning," he said, "Fulbert—" He stooped and again caught Guibert by the shoulder.

"Did Fulbert give you that money this morning?"

Guibert shook his head. "Not this morning. Tonight."

"What for?"

Guibert smiled happily. "I didn't do it." He pulled out the parchment packet from his breast. "I didn't give it to him in his posset. He was asleep anyhow. I only opened the door."

"Oh, my God," said Thibault and was off like a greyhound down the street, Foulques after him. The moon had gone down, and Foulques tripped twice, but hardly waited to be on his feet before he ran on. Down the Rue des Marmousets they ran, then sharp to the right into the Rue Cocatrice, to the left into the Rue St. Christophe, through the narrow Rue des Oïes into the Rue Neuve Notre Dame, and so breathless round the corner into the Place du Parvis. Even as they darted into the Place, it seemed to them that two shadows slipped under the overhang of the Maison du Saumon into the ruelle to the Rue Sainte Marine.

"There!" Thibault jerked out and swung sharp to the left in pursuit. With a desperate effort Foulques pitched forward and caught his arm.

"Abelard," he gasped, jerking his head to the house behind them. "He's maybe dying."

With a snap like a dog, Thibault turned and darted back across the Parvis. The house was dark and shuttered, but when they reached it, they found the door an inch ajar. They passed inside, and the Parvis was silent again. Then a crack of light gleamed through the chink in the topmost shutter, feet came pounding down the stair, and Thibault dashed through the door, alone, shouting with crying. It was to the porter's lodge into the Cloître Notre Dame that he ran, and then his hands were on the hammer beside the bell, and the wild clatter of it filled the Parvis. The door opened and he plunged through it, almost overturning the bewildered porter, and on to the archway where hung the great bell of the schools. Cursing and sobbing as he pulled on the rope, it was some solace to him to hear its huge voice drown his own, and clamor his cry for vengeance over the Cloister and the sleeping island, and across the river to the silent Quartier. Windows opened, voices questioned and cried out, feet tramped and ran, all the diverse whispering and crackling

of dry timber before the roar of the conflagration leaps
to the dark sky, and drowns all individual hates.

Only two souls on the island gave it no heed: Peter
Abelard in his high room, moaning half conscious on his
pillow; and the figure holding its knees and rocking to
and fro on the doorstep by the house in the Rue des
Marmousets, empty now, for Roger and Bele Alys had
long ago rushed out, seeing him not at all in their haste.
It was some while before anyone remembered him, for
Thibault's mind was on the two shadows he had seen
slipping under the overhang by the Maison du Saumon,
and the hunt went to the north of the island. They
started one hare, but it took sanctuary: whoever it was
had the key of the canons' door. One man leapt from the
parapet into the river, but whether the rat swam or
drowned it was too dark to see. The third they ran to
earth, crouching in the underground passage to the river
steps at the Port St. Landry, and it was a little while before they were finished with him. Dawn was breaking as
they came down the Rue des Marmousets, faintly dis-
coloring their flaring torches and what they carried in
their hands. Their noise had lessened to a kind of con-
fused snarling, but though it swelled again to a keener
note when the foremost among them saw their quarry,
he made no attempt to run. He did not even look up
when they reached him. However, though he gave them
less sport than the other, they had their will with this
one also.

CHAPTER IV

FOR three days sciatica had kept Gilles de Vannes in bed: today his progress across the Parvis was still painful enough. The sweat broke on him as he climbed the stairs to Abelard's lodging. He stood outside the door for a while, mopping his brow and getting his breath, thrusting out his underlip meantime at the crowd of young men that hung about the landing whispering and watching. For Abelard's quiet, they had him still in the inner room, but to Gilles, as he came into the outer room, it seemed that he might as well be in the Parvis, with the coming and going and the confusion of tongues. He walked through the crowd, scowling, and recognizing no one. The door to Abelard's room was closed: he was glad of that, at least, and a young giant that he did not know sat with his back to it, a young face, but sullen and brooding.

"I am glad," said Gilles, "that one man in Paris has got some common sense."

Thibault looked up at him. "I don't let anybody in but what he says," said he. "And if they make too much noise out here, I throw them out."

Gilles looked at the young man. Those eyes were haunted by something beyond grief. Thibault felt some warmth of human kindness reach him, the first time for three days.

"Is there anyone in with him now?"

"Just Foulques. He's asleep. But he said you were to see him, any time you came."

[212]

"It was you that found him," said Gilles, stating a fact.

"And Foulques," amended Thibault. He got up. "Will you hold your noise," said he to the room at large, "till I open the door?"

Then fell a silence. Gilles steeled his coward's heart. He went through the door that the young man opened for him, swung back the arras, and stood looking towards the bed.

He knew that Abelard was not asleep, but so long as he chose to pretend he was, Gilles was content to wait. A thin dark lad sitting by the bed rose. The two looked at one another, and at the silent command in Gilles's eye, the boy nodded and went out.

"I counted on you doing that," said a cool voice from the bed.

Gilles grunted. He walked over to it, and sat down on the chest from which Foulques had risen. He was still scowling as his eye met Abelard's, and the other frowned back.

"I suppose they've told you that I'm going to live?" the cool light voice went on.

Gilles nodded.

"Have they begun to joke yet, Gilles?"

"Not yet," said Gilles. "So far, it has been more like the Weeping Wall of Jerusalem."

"Three days is a long time," said Abelard thoughtfully. "I doubt if I should have had the decency to keep off it so long, if—if it had been friend Alberic of Rheims, for instance, instead of me." His voice cracked on the name, but he finished well enough. "By the way," he went on, "this must be a high day for Alberic. It's the first of October, St. Rémy, isn't it? Do you know how they

keep the feast at Rheims, Gilles? You go to a church
with a herring behind you on a string, and the point is
to step on the herring of the man in front, and keep your
herring from the advances of the man behind. I'd give
a good deal to see Alberic take part in that procession.
Or have I muddled it? Is it some day in Lent?"

The brittle voice was very near being intolerable.
Gilles sat silent.

"You are hard to amuse today, Gilles."

"Stop that," said Gilles.

The bright eyes from the bed watched him inimically,
then suddenly darkened.

Gilles dropped his head on the hand that lay on the
coverlet. "Would God I had died for thee, O Absalom,
my son, my son."

It was a long time before either spoke. At last Abelard
heaved a great sigh, as though he had dropped a heavy
load.

"I was lost for you, Gilles. I have lied, and lied, and
lied."

"I could come no sooner, Peter. I could not get out
of my bed: and you know I am ill to carry."

Abelard's eyes caressed him. "They told me. There's
nothing they have not told me, these last three days. Being a sick man is like being a log caught in a stream,
Gilles. All the straws gather round it."

"Please God, you won't be a sick man long," said Gilles.

Abelard's mouth tightened. "I shan't be it here, anyhow. As soon as they can move me, I am going to St.
Denis."

"St. Denis? You might have chosen a quieter place,"
said Gilles. "If you want monks' nursing, and they're

[214]

good nurses enough, you'd be as well looked after, and a deal quieter, at St. Germain."

"You see, I am taking the vows at St. Denis," said Abelard. "Abbot Adam says that in my case it will be only a nominal novitiate."

There came from Gilles no sound but a kind of strangled crow. Wrath and stupefaction were choking him. He dropped Abelard's hand, and heaved himself to his feet. Abelard lay with half-closed eyes, watching him. At last Gilles spoke.

"If I had the power, Peter," he said, "I should have you kidnaped and kept prisoner till God was pleased to restore you to your reason."

"I knew you would say that," said Abelard. He closed his eyes and frowned a little, as if trying to marshal his arguments.

"Sit down, Gilles. I want to tell you the truth. I do not want to be a monk. I have not any vocation. I want to go on fighting and teaching the way I have always done. But that is ended."

"It is not ended," Gilles broke out. "You say this because you are a sick man, but when your strength comes back and you are your own man again—"

Abelard's eyes looked at him through narrowed lids.

"I am not a man now," he said. "I am a kind of monster. You go home and read the *Attis* again, Gilles, and some of Martial: and then read the passages in Leviticus and Deuteronomy, about the kind of thing I am now. And how, with that knowledge in me, do you suppose I am to rule the Schools? I'd shrivel in my chair and stammer at the first snigger."

"You would do nothing of the sort," said Gilles

fiercely. "And there'd be plenty—like your giant at the door there—to put the snigger, along with a good many teeth, down the sniggerer's throat."

"It's a good ox," said Abelard indifferently. "Nephew to your old friend, Thibault of Champagne. But fists are a poor reply to a gibe. And I've never yet heard the joke that turned the tables on that particular jest."

Gilles drew in his underlip and scowled at the figure on the bed. The man lying there was not fit for argument: but once he had made up his mind, there would be no turning him. Gilles knew it of old. He made his last brutal throw.

"I did not know you were a coward."

"No more did I," said Abelard tranquilly. "But I do now. It is supposed, I believe, to be the inevitable consequence. But see here, Gilles," he spoke with a shade more vehemence, "I have laughed at too many people myself to stand being laughed at now. I don't say I haven't been gibed at—but so far I had the sharper tongue of the two."

Gilles was silent. He knew the Schools: and he knew there was no quarter.

"Suppose," he began, "that you do not make up your mind now; that you go for a while to Brittany—"

"For God's sake," said Abelard. His arm was across his eyes and he was shuddering with the sobbing that he would not let break out. And with a moment of clairvoyance, Gilles saw the place that he had never seen: a cart track to the river and coming down it the figure of a girl. He groaned and dropped his head in his hands.

It was Abelard who spoke first.

"I want to tell you, Gilles. It has to be. I think I have always known it would be. That queer terror—" He broke off. "I knew it once, riding down to Brittany with—" He stopped again. "And here, reading Ezekiel, before I went to Fulbert and said I would marry her. And before that, long before that. Do you remember when I came back from Brittany, after my mother took the veil, and though they offered me the Schools here, I went to sit under old Anselm at Laon, and read theology? You teased me then, do you remember?"—he creased his eyes at Gilles, affectionately. *"Philosophy is my washpot: over theology also will I cast out my shoe.* I suppose there was something of that in it too. But it was a kind of bargain. I thought if I went one mile I—I would not be asked to go twain."

Gilles listened. With his mind he accepted, but he had nothing in his experience to give him understanding.

"I suppose it's like Saul on the road to Damascus," Abelard went on. "And I've been kicking long enough against the pricks. Long enough to be lamed for life, anyhow." He laughed a little. "Only . . . he saw a great light before he went blind. I haven't seen much yet. Barring Fulbert's face when they wakened me."

Gilles sat sunken, his head in his hands.

"Origen was no monk," he said at last.

Abelard nodded. "But I'm no Origen." In a little while —"All the same, they're making me very welcome at St. Denis. I have never had so many civil things said to me in my life."

"They know they'll be the talk of Christendom," said Gilles bitterly. "What's the tombs of the kings to putting their cowl on Peter Abelard?"

"And they are taking me with no patrimony," Abelard

went on. "I told Abbot Adam I must make whatever provision I had for—for my wife."

Gilles looked up startled. "What is to become of her?"

"She is taking the veil at Argenteuil."

Gilles again rose to his feet.

"Listen to me, Peter Abelard. This is no way to speak to a sick man, but I must do it. Bury yourself alive, if you must. But must you bury her alive too?"

Abelard's face had become a fine-drawn mask.

"She is willing," he said quietly.

"Of course she is willing. She would go through hell if you bade her. But had you any right to bid her?"

"What could she do?" said Abelard defiantly. "What kind of world is this for a woman that has no kin of her own, and a husband, if you call him a husband, in the cloister?"

"What is to hinder her going to your sister, with her boy?"

Abelard winced, and was silent. Suddenly he turned on Gilles, eyes that looked up from such a pit of pain, that Gilles's heart turned over.

"Because, if you want the truth, I could not stand it. Because I am jealous of every man that looks at her. Because I could not endure to see her kiss even Hugh the Stranger. And that was when I was a man. Now—" He had broken at last. The sobs were tearing out of him.

Gilles stood over him, grasping his shoulders, his anger turned to an agony of compassion.

"Peter, forgive me," he said. "I was blind. O my son, as if she would not have given her body to the wolves rather than you should suffer one tithe of what I have made you suffer now."

In a little while, Abelard lay quiet.

"I'm glad you got the truth out of me, Gilles," he said. "I was lying, even to myself, before."

Moving clumsily, but with amazing efficiency, Gilles got a basin of water and bathed his flushed face.

"Could you sleep, if I sat here for a while and kept the rest out?"

Abelard nodded. At that moment, the door opened and Foulques's diffident head came round it.

"Sir, it's the Abbot Adam of St. Denis."

Abelard lay for a moment with closed eyes.

"Ask him to come in." He opened them and looked up at Gilles.

"God bless you, Gilles. But I must go my own way."

BOOK IV
THE PARACLETE

August 1121–November 1122

CHAPTER I

"Have you read the *De Trinitate*, Gilles?"

Gilles nodded. "It is more than his accusers have, I'll be bound."

"And is it heretical?"

"Of course it is heretical. Every book that ever was written about the Trinity is heretical, barring the Athanasian Creed. And even that only saves itself by contradicting everything it says as fast as it says it."

Pierre de Montboissier flung back his head and laughed delightedly. It was four years since he had heard anyone talk like this.

"Not but what Abelard does the same," went on Gilles thoughtfully. "But there is too wide a space between the assertion and the contradiction for a porker like Alberic to carry it in his head. He gets his nose under one gate, and squeals there. Friend Alberic and t'other animal that's coupled with him had it spread all over Soissons that Abelard taught there were three Gods. And the last news of the trial is that he is going to be charged with saying there is only one, but three ways of looking at Him."

"Sabellianism?" said Pierre.

Gilles nodded approvingly. "Good lad," said he. He chuckled. "I'd give one of my few remaining years to be at the council, and watch old Palestrina dodging when the great words go flying about, for fear one hits him and he'd have to explain it. It wasn't his theology that made him Papal Legate: and he must be cursing the luck that set him to judge a trial for heresy. He has as good a head for politics as any man I know, and near as good a palate as myself, and he and King Louis have the same tastes in jokes: but as for judging Trinity in Unity and Unity in Trinity, he must be wishing himself back in Italy."

"But tell me, Gilles, how does it come that Master Peter is being tried in Soissons, and before the Archbishop of Rheims, as well as Canon of Palestrina? Surely Abelard as a monk of St. Denis should come under the jurisdiction of Paris, and therefore of Sens? If anyone were going to summon him, it should have been his own archbishop, and not Ralph of Rheims?"

Gilles looked at him mournfully. "They've got you, Pierre," he said whimsically. "The mountains may depart and the hills be removed, but to every man his own diocesan, and let no bishop trespass on his neighbor's see."

Pierre flushed.

"There, I was only teasing you," said Gilles. "And the man who will be the next abbot of Cluny—you need not shake your head, for I know it—will have less need of Virgil than of canon law.

> "'A boy I can remember used to sing
> All the long summer days: but now the songs,
> The very songs he sang are all forgotten.
> The voice has fled the singer: all are fled.'

But don't forget them altogether, Pierre. 'O Lord, by these things men live.' "

The young man sat silent. "Life is easier if one forgets, Gilles."

"May God forgive you," said Gilles. "But there," he caught himself up, "the man who has found that out is the man who will never forget. Repent, if you like, Pierre. But never forget."

Pierre got up and walked over to the hearth. He stood there, his arm on the chimney, and his head resting on it. Something in his attitude brought back to Gilles too many memories.

"Bring me that litter from the window, Pierre," he said abruptly. "There are some letters that I want to show you." And as the young man roused, gladly enough, and crossed the room, "Teasing aside, you raised a very interesting point about Sens, and only that Abelard was pawing the ground for a fight, I believe the whole business could have been quashed. But you see, he has been teaching in Champagne: and though it was in a priory of St. Denis, part of Champagne comes under the jurisdiction of Rheims."

"When did he leave St. Denis?"

"Just as soon as St. Denis could get decently quit of him," said Gilles grimly. "They had made one vast mistake. They thought our Peter was a man of easy morals. Which at no time of his life was true of him." Gilles's eyes slid momentarily sideways. "And they counted on harnessing a great reputation for their cloister, and, barring certain disabilities, a good boon companion in their pleasures. And behold, said Abbot Adam, I'd as soon have housed Bernard himself."

Pierre laughed in spite of himself. "What possessed him to go there, Gilles? Did he not know what a den it was?"

"Abelard knew less about other people than anyone

[225]

I've ever known," said Gilles. "He thought about things. He only knew it as the first abbey in France. And I think it was the first place came to his mind to hide his head in." He was silent for a while. "So they took advantage of the hordes of young men that besieged the Abbey, to send him off to their priory near Provins to teach in peace. It emptied Paris, but Abbot Adam cared little for that. Only it began to empty Rheims, and that got friend Alberic on the raw."

"So it was Alberic," said Pierre slowly.

"You remember Alberic?"

"I do. I suppose all that was four years ago. Do you remember, Gilles, I nearly hit him? I wish now I had. So he planned a heresy hunt?"

"Not at first. There were rumblings, of course. But the real pinch is that Alberic has a poor head for logic. If they ask him a question, he has to get two days' notice, and meantime the little Lombard lawyer fellow looks it up for him. And Abelard has gone on from reasoning about the kinds and species to reasoning about theology. It is true he has a good many of the Fathers behind him. But Alberic quotes the Blessed Gregory, and St. Ambrose, that theology is to be believed, and not to be discussed."

"And Abelard?"

"You'll see his broadside there. '*To a certain one ignorant of dialectic.*' He named no names: but it has gone like a spark in dry grass."

Pierre picked it up and leaved it over, his eye kindling as he read. " '*The age of miracles is past: but the war goes on. If we cannot convince by miracles, we must by words. And is not Christ Himself the Word, the Logos, from which our study, our logic, is derived? Moreover, did He not Himself convince the Jews in frequent argument, and build up the faith not only by the power of miracles, but by the potency of words? . . . Reason has more force with the discriminating than miracles, for it is debatable whether miracles may not be brought about by diabolic illusion.'*"

He whistled. "*'Above all is logic essential for such doctors as, confident that they have some skill in resolving questions, do not simply shuffle from under them.'* Can't you hear his very voice in that *subterfugium?*" He looked down again at the sheet of parchment. "Is that his seal? It is a beautiful one."

"It is," said Gilles, non-committal.

Pierre had taken it over to the window. Gilles's eye followed him. He saw his shoulders stiffen.

"It is a tolerable likeness," Gilles went on. "Though better of Heloise than of himself. He had it made from his own drawing, when she was first in Brittany. And he uses it still."

"I thought I recognized the face," said Pierre quietly.

"You are not the only one," said Gilles. He looked among the parchments in his lap. "There's a pretty letter here from that old fox Roscelin. *'And the seal wherewith you have signed your stinking letter is proof enough of the ardor with which you burn towards her still.'*"

"What right has Roscelin to speak of her?"

Gilles shrugged his shoulders. "It is not the end of his civilities. The dowry that Abelard gave with her to Argenteuil he describes as his reward to his harlot for past prostitution, since similar pleasure in the present was not to be looked for."

Pierre stood silent, biting his under-lip.

"You are new to the amenities of controversy," said Gilles. "But hear the conclusion. *'I am in some perplexity how to address this letter. Clerk you are not, for you have taken the cowl: monk you are not, for you have assumed the doctor: layman you are not, for behold your tonsure. There remains the name of Peter: yet Peter is the name of a man.'*"

"May God damn him," said Pierre, very low.

"One council did, to begin with," said Gilles equably, "a good many years ago. It is the spite of the tailless fox: he would have Peter branded too. By the way, that same council was likewise held at Soissons. Soissons is a good place for a heresy hunt. It's not so long since they had a couple of decent poor burghers up for Manichaeism: they were in the bishop's ward, but the crowd got at them and burnt one of them alive. What kind of monster they thought a Manichee was, I do not know: but they roasted him anyhow. And by the time Abelard rode in to attend the Council, they were ready to stone him in the streets. I think they would have, only for that young ox of a Thibault, riding behind him."

"How did they get their council summoned?"

"Ask Alberic and Lotulf. First of all they barked that he had no master's license: but that fell flat, for the man who had ruled the Schools of Paris might surely teach in a country priory. By the way, they ate the countryside before them, his youngsters: they say it was like a swarm of locusts: you couldn't buy so much as an egg in Provins market. Then they said that he was lecturing on the pagan poets as well as on the Fathers, but that was a stale herring too. And then Abelard played into their hands. Their enemy wrote a book. Here it is."

Pierre fastened on it. He turned over the pages, murmuring phrases to himself, now and then glancing up to share them with Gilles. " '*God the Father, Power: God the Son, Wisdom: God the Holy Ghost, Love . . . and this in a measure was revealed unto Plato, when he conceived his doctrine of the soul of the world.*' That must have roused friend Alberic. Listen, Gilles," he broke into sudden laughter, "*homo navigabilis, risibilis*—isn't it like him that the first human qualities he thinks of are that a man can laugh and can manage a boat?" He read on, his face softening.

" '*If a man desire to understand God, let him prepare himself for that understanding by good life, and let him take the way of humility, for by that road alone may he come nigh that height of intellectual vision. Not indeed that he will ever attain thereto, so long as he is in this mortal flesh: for there shall no man see Him, and live. . . . And concerning the mystery of the Trinity we make no promise to teach the final truth, which neither we nor any mortal can know, but at best some likeness of it, some neighbor to it in human reason. . . . And so, whatever we may set forth concerning this most high philosophy, we declare it to be a shadow, not the truth.*' " He laid down the book, transfigured. "There is no one like him, Gilles. But how dare they, after reading that, bring him to trial?"

"I do not imagine for a moment that they have read it," said Gilles placidly. "The first paragraph or so would be enough. Alberic leapt in the air at the suggestion that Plato might have been aware of the Holy Ghost, forgetting that St. Paul would probably have agreed. They dashed off to good old Archbishop Ralph, dining with his Eminence the Legate. Ralph knows as much about Plato as would cover his great toe, but he did know that Rheims was thin of scholars: the Legate did not even know that, but he has his instructions from His Holiness to humor the French clergy as much as possible, and presumably he took it that Abelard was in a minority. So a council was convened at Soissons."

"And Abelard summoned to attend?"

"Invited, rather. His Eminence is a good diplomatist." Gilles began to chuckle. "So the moment Abelard arrives, he goes straight to wait on his Eminence, presents him with his book, begs him to read it, and declares that if he has written anything contrary to the Catholic faith, he is prepared to make any correction or satisfaction that is demanded."

"That is very like him. Well? Did Palestrina read it?"

"The last man that saw Palestrina reading a book— But he soon recovered himself, and told Peter to take it to the Archbishop and his two accusers, since it was they who had brought the charge. It struck Abelard as an odd proceeding that the prosecutors were also to be the judges. On the other hand, he reflected that they had probably omitted to read the book. So he presented them with a copy of it. Oh, our friend is enjoying himself. You need waste no pity on him. And they have turned it upside down and inside out to find the cocatrice-egg, and meantime the council drags on—you know the usual formulae, *De vita et honestate clericorum* and so forth. And Abelard settled down to give a course of public lectures, and in a day or two the town was at his feet."

"How long will it sit?"

"This week should see it ended. Geoffrey of Chartres—"

"Is Geoffrey there?"

"He is, thank God. He saw to that. Geoffrey is certain of victory. And so is Abelard. Especially after what happened on Sunday. I had it from Geoffrey himself. At long last—you know, all this time Abelard's name has never been so much as mentioned in the council—Alberic comes to see Abelard, very bland, with a handful of his scholars, all bursting with excitement but all very civil, Alberic rubbing his hands and hoping Master Peter is comfortable in his lodging; and then he begins to talk about the book and the excellence of its style, and behind him the pack all wagging their sterns and panting, but not a yelp out of them yet, and their eyes all fixed on their master.

" 'One thing I noted in your book that a little surprised me,' says Alberic, 'that although God begat God, and is but one, you nevertheless deny that God begat Himself.'

" 'That is so,' says Abelard. 'And if you wish, I shall be happy to explain the reason.'

"The word 'reason' was enough. The pack gave a kind of yelp. 'We care not for human reason,' says Alberic grandly, 'nor our own interpretation of the sense in matters such as this: we ask only for the word of authority.'

" 'Precisely,' says Master Peter. 'Turn the page, and you will find the authority.'

"Alberic fumbles, and Abelard reaches for the book and finds it for him, St. Augustine, *De Trinitate*. Book I. Chapter I. '*Whoso attributes to God the power of be-*

*getting Himself, is the more in error because it is not so,
not only in respect of God, but of all creatures, corporeal
or spiritual: for there is nothing whatever that begets itself.'* The pack stopped wagging their sterns and their
eyes got anxious. The sweat broke on Alberic, but he
managed to stammer something.

" 'It must,' says he, 'be rightly interpreted.'

" 'I heartily agree with you,' says Abelard lightly, 'but
that, after all, is nothing to the point, since what you
asked of me was not the sense of the passage, but the
words only. If, however, you care to consider the sense
and the interpretation, I shall be happy to explain to you
how on your own showing you have yourself fallen into
that heresy which declares that the Father is His own
son.' "

"If I had been there!" sighed Pierre. "Well?"

"Not so good," said Gilles, his eyes darkening. "For
our porker turned into a wild boar and took himself off,
threatening all manner, and vowing that neither his rea-
sons nor his authorities would stand Abelard in stead by
the time he was done with him."

"But they'll laugh him out of court," said Pierre.

"As our friend Peter says in that book you have there,
most men are animal and not spiritual. And the bishops'
bench at Rheims is in no way remarkable for intelligence.
But there's Geoffrey. I do not think there will be much
miscarriage of justice so long as he is there. I'm dry with
talking, Pierre. Pour me out a drink, and another for
yourself."

Pierre walked over to the dresser. "Angers? Or Bordeaux?"

"Bordeaux, I think. It's chilly, to be August. Well, I give you a toast, Pierre. Chartres!"

"Chartres!" said Pierre solemnly, and raised his goblet. He stopped, the rim at his lips. "There's someone on the stair, speaking to Jehan."

A low imperious voice, a little impatient: Jehan's slow foot hurrying in spite of himself.

"Light the candles, Pierre," said Gilles. He was shaking. The door opened and Jehan looked round it.

"My Lord of Chartres," he growled.

Pierre turned from the fire, the candles in his hand, his eyes shining. Gilles heaved himself out of his chair, and took a step or two. The arras swung, and a tall figure came through the doorway.

"You're welcome, Geoffrey. Good news travels fast—" He stopped, for the candlelight had fallen on Geoffrey's face.

Mechanically, Pierre de Montboissier moved over to the table and set the candles down upon it, very carefully. He even busied himself trimming the wick of one of them that hung over. And still Geoffrey did not speak.

"So they've damned him," said Gilles.

Geoffrey nodded. He was haggard with fatigue, and his lips gray with dust. Pierre poured out a goblet and brought it to him, his hands trembling. The tired eyes noted it, traveled up to the young wretched face; and the bitter mouth relaxed into a smile of astonishing sweetness.

"Don't fret, lad," he said. "We'll have it annulled. That is why I rode so fast. I was determined I would see the Archbishop at Sens before they did."

[233]

He took a long drink, still standing, and then sat down, stretching his long legs in front of him.

"It might be worse, Gilles. When I saw how it was going I told him to make no protest, but submit to whatever they chose to demand. His book is burnt, and he is sent for penance to St. Médard."

"St. Médard!" It broke from Pierre almost like a howl. "But it's the penitentiary for all France!"

"I know. I know." Again the tired eyes rested on Pierre's angry face, as though they eased their pain in that passionate loyalty. "But it will not be a penitentiary for him. They have a new abbot, Geoffrey of the Stag Neck: and if I know him, he'll receive his prisoner like a prince-bishop, instead of a penitent."

"It is more than his Prior will do," said Gilles, speaking for the first time, his voice at its harshest. "Maybe you have forgotten that he is the pious youngster we used to call the Blessed Gosvin."

Geoffrey opened his mouth to speak and shut it. His brows knit.

"You're right, Gilles. I never thought of him. I thought that he was at Anchin."

"He has the reputation, I believe, of being very efficacious in dealing with the refractory," went on Gilles. "That is why he was transferred from his own abbey to the stonier ground at St. Médard."

Pierre de Montboissier got to his feet. He was looking at Geoffrey with cold hatred.

"I think I had better be going, sir," he said to Gilles. "They think better of Master Peter at Cluny than they seem to do here. And the sooner I get back with the news, the better. They will maybe stir themselves a little for his release." The young voice cracked dangerously. He stooped to take Gilles's hand, but a long arm shot out, gripped his shoulder in a vise and swung him round.

"So you think I flung him to the wolves?" said the tired voice. The grip suddenly relaxed, and he leant back, his hand over his eyes. "And perhaps you're right, young Pierre. Perhaps you're right."

The young man stood irresolute. He saw the statesman's mask, furrowed with disappointment, the heavy line from nose to chin, the droop of the rigid mouth: and from that his eyes traveled to the riding-boots, white with dust. This man had been in the saddle for twelve hours, and for no other end than that which he in his arrogance had claimed.

"Forgive me, sir," he said. "I think I was beside myself. I—" he hesitated. "Whatever you did, it was—it was for Master Peter."

"For God's sake give me a drink and sit down," said Gilles. "And maybe, Geoffrey, if this malapert would pour you out another, you would rouse yourself from your private reflections, and tell us what did happen."

Geoffrey's face relaxed into a sudden smile. He stretched out his arms in a long yawn, and stooping forward began to struggle with his boots. In a flash Pierre was on his knees, his hands on the heel. The older man made no protest. "Indeed, it is a Christian act, lad," said he, "for I am so stiff I can hardly straighten my knees."

Gilles had got out of his chair and was busy carving at the dresser.

"There's a cold partridge here, Geoffrey, and whatever Pierre left of a venison pasty. It is a poor welcome

we have given an over-ridden man, but you will bear
us no grudge."

Geoffrey reached for the platter gratefully, but after
a few mouthfuls he pushed it from him.

"I'll get rid of my load first," said he. "You had my
letter?"

Gilles nodded. "We were talking of it, even as you
came. What turned the tide? You thought it was flowing pretty strongly, then."

"And so I did, as late as yesterday at noon. I tell you,
before stupidity the gods themselves are dumb. If it
weren't a tragedy this precious council was as good a
farce as any mime ever played."

He paused a moment, arranging his memories.

"It began with a kind of informal meeting in the
chapter-house, yesterday morning, before the Council
sat. Palestrina has no great intelligence—*subintellex*, Peter
Abelard calls him—but he has a good deal of common
sense; and he asked them pretty sharply why they had
prevailed on him to summon a council to judge a heretic,
and from that day to this there had not been so much as
a cheep out of them, and neither the man's name nor his
book ever mentioned. Had they found anything to question, or had they not? Alberic got up and stammered
out a few things: I kept my eye on him, and he got red
about the ears, contradicted himself, and sat down. There
was some whispering and nudging, and at last I got up.

" 'My Lords,' said I, 'you know the quality of this
man's teaching, you know his genius. You know that
whatever he chooses to study, he so draws men after him
that he has outstripped the fame of the men who were his
masters and ours, and like a vine his branches have spread

from sea to sea. If you should—as I trust not—condemn him unheard, you know that you will outrage many, and that there are not a few who will come to his defense: above all, since we see nothing in this present book which demands any kind of open censure: remembering too that saying of Jerome's, "It is the strong who have most enemies: it is on the mountain peaks that the thunderbolts fall." Look to it that violence on your part does not but increase his fame, and that we do not find ourselves credited with jealousy, rather than justice. A slander, as that great doctor of the Church again reminds us, is soon crushed: and the future is the judge of the past. If, on the other hand, you are minded to follow the canonical procedure, let his accusers bring forward one dogma or one script which is indubitably his, let him be questioned upon it, and given freedom to reply: so that if convicted or brought to confusion, he may hereafter hold his peace: and herein follow the counsel of the blessed Nicodemus when he said, *"Doth our law judge any man before it hear him and know what he doeth?"* ' "

"There is more of Ulysses in you than Nicodemus, Geoffrey," said Gilles. "Well?"

"That roused them," said Geoffrey, smiling in retrospect. "If they had been silent before, they were noisy enough now. 'Rare advice, surely,' they shouted, 'for the like of us to controvert with him, when the whole world could not stand against his sophistries and his arguing!'

" 'Doubtless,' said I, 'the Sanhedrim felt something of the same diffidence in the case I have mentioned.' "

Gilles sighed. "I fear you were wasted on them, Geoffrey. Well?"

Geoffrey's face clouded. "The thing was hopeless.

[237]

Nothing would induce them to give him a hearing. They knew, Alberic anyhow, that he would make them a laughing-stock. So I made my final move. I said that after all perhaps they were right: that we were few indeed to try a matter of such serious import, and that the case demanded much more prolonged examination than was in our power to give. So therefore I would now suggest that judgment be postponed: that the accused should be taken back to his own abbey of St. Denis by his abbot, whom we had the good fortune to see amongst us: and there, might be convened an assembly more numerous and more expert than ourselves, and the case be submitted to their closer examination."

"Superb," said Gilles. He had forgotten the issue, in sheer delight at the technique. But Pierre de Montboissier sat looking at the ground, his eyes unlit.

"It swept the board," said Geoffrey. "Palestrina's gasp of relief was like the spouting of a whale. Before they had time to think, he had put it to them and was on his feet, bidding them attend him to the Mass of the Holy Ghost that would open the final meeting of the Council: and passing me he bade me—it's a good-hearted soul— to go to Peter Abelard and tell him he was free to return to St. Denis, and there await further consideration. I was glad enough of the errand. But if I had known—" He got to his feet and came over to the fire, holding out his hands to it as if suddenly cold.

"You are chilled after sweating with your riding," said Gilles. "Put another log on the fire, Pierre."

"It is not that," said Geoffrey. He straightened himself, and stood looking at Pierre de Montboissier.

"Well. I attended Palestrina on his way to robe him-

[238]

self, and then I came away. I saw Alberic and Lotulf whispering in the cloister, but I thought nothing of it. Natural enough that the hounds should snarl when the stag has taken to the water. I did not wait long with Abelard—he was lodging in St. Jean des Vignes close by— postponed our merry-making till that night when the Council would have risen. I came back, thinking I would listen to the Mass of the Holy Ghost with a deal more devotion than I had so far. Just as I reached the cathedral cloister, I saw Alberic and Lotulf come out of the sacristy door. They spoke a moment, then Lotulf went across to the singing-school and Alberic hurried in. But I had seen their faces. I made all the speed I could: but just as I got to the sacristy door, I heard the roar of the organ. I was too late. The procession had begun."

He sat down again and covered his face with his hands.

"*Exsurgat Deus—Let God arise and let His enemies be scattered.* If ever a man committed the sin against the Holy Ghost, it was myself listening there. Palestrina's little secretary was fidgeting about, laying by the robes, and I seized on him. He used to be a scholar of Master Peter's, long ago, when he taught at St. Geneviève, and he had listened with all his ears. The pair of foxes had cornered old Ralph. They had told him he would be the laughing-stock of France if he suffered the matter to go beyond his jurisdiction: that Paris would fight for her men against Rheims: that he was Primate of France, and was Rheims to go to school to Paris to learn theology and canon law? And with that, old Ralph, all his hackles up, charges down on Palestrina. Palestrina, it seems, showed some fight: but with a good deal of to and fro, it was agreed that without further discussion Peter Abelard was to be condemned because he had lectured in public upon, and had put into circulation, a book that had received the imprimatur neither of the Roman Pontiff nor of the Church: that the example would be of great avail to the faith and a warning against similar presumption in future. The book was to be burned: and Abelard committed to perpetual imprisonment in St. Médard."

He was silent again. Pierre had moved into the shadow behind the chimney, and had turned his face to the wall.

"There was nothing to be done but let the farce play itself out. I hurried back to Abelard."

Again he stopped.

"I told him with all the force I could that he had better submit. That violence on his part would only mean . . . God knows what humiliation. You know that yourself, Pierre."

There came a muffled assent.

"Technically they were in their rights, and Abelard had promised at the beginning to abide by the Legate's decision. Let him take his sentence, and I swore to him on my honor that by the morning France would be ringing with it. They would be taken in their own net, branded for the jealous dunces that they were. As for perpetual imprisonment, Palestrina had been driven to it, and in a day or two, once he was clear of Rheims, would give the order for his release. I had only time to say it, when the summons came from the Council, for Abelard."

Again the silence fell. Gilles's eyes were fixed on the darkness beyond the candlelight. He saw the serried faces in their stalls, complacent and greedy for the show; Palestrina flushed and angry with himself and everybody

else: Alberic sleek in his doctor's robes. He saw the bra-
zier of burning charcoal. But the solitary figure standing
by it he would not see.

"Well, he burnt his book." Geoffrey laughed shortly.
"And to make the farce complete, while it was crackling
there, and not a sound in all the cathedral, one of the
fools standing by mutters that he thought he had seen
in the book that God the Father alone was omnipotent.
Palestrina pricked up his ears; anything to ease that old
seared politician's conscience of his. 'Surely you are mistaken,' he booms out, 'for every schoolboy knows better
than that. For it is the common article of faith to hold
and profess that there are three omnipotents.' "

"Good God," said Gilles, under his breath.

Geoffrey looked at him under his eyebrows and
nodded.

"There was a squeak of laughter somewhere at the
back, and then a horrid silence. And then my own
familiar devil, Thierry of Chartres, says, as if to himself,
but in just that intoning chant of the creed that carries
to every corner of the cathedral, '*Yet are there not three
omnipotents, but one Omnipotent.*' "

"That would help Abelard's cause," said Gilles grimly.

"I thought Palestrina would have a seizure," said
Geoffrey, "and as Thierry's bishop, I called him to order
pretty fiercely, but Thierry's blood was up: after all,
he is a Breton himself.

" 'O fools,' he shouted, 'that neither know nor seek the
truth, and have condemned a son of Israel. Return to
judgment and judge the judge himself, that ye chose for
the instruction of faith and the correction of error, for
out of his own mouth is he condemned. By God's mercy,

[241]

as once Susanna was delivered from her accusers, set this innocent man free!' "

Pierre's eyes in the dark of the chimney corner shone like a wolf's.

"By that time, I think the only man unmoved was Abelard himself. He stood there, like a man in stone, watching his parchments burn. Then old Ralph heaves himself up, to save his Eminence's face, for Palestrina was past speech.

" 'In very truth, my Lord,' says he, 'the Father is omnipotent, the Son is omnipotent, and the Holy Ghost is omnipotent, and whoever dissents from this, he hath erred and gone out of the way. But now, if it please you, it were well that our brother should expound his faith in presence of us all, that it may be approved or corrected as shall be just and right.' I could see Alberic's jaw drop, for this was not according to plan.

"Ralph sat down, looking at Peter, but Peter gave no sign of having heard. I do not think he had. 'Speak, my son,' says the old man, leaning forward. Peter looked up at him, dazed. 'Speak, my son,' says he again."

Geoffrey stopped.

"It was Lazarus come back from the dead. If you have seen despair when it begins to hope—I could have risen in my seat and shouted, for I knew the day was ours if he once began to speak. But so did Alberic. He was muttering in the Archbishop's ear, and the old man rises again to his feet and makes a motion to Peter to wait.

" 'My son,' says he, 'all that is required of you is that you shall but make the profession of your faith in the words of the Athanasian Creed.'

"I saw Peter's hands begin to shake, but he made no

[242]

sign. He stood up there before them all, his face like a mask.

" '*Quicunque vult*,' he began, but his throat was dry, and he had to swallow once or twice. And suddenly there was Alberic's smile beside him, and the pudgy hand holding out the book, as you might to a stumbling choir-boy, open at the Creed. I had prayed for nothing since I sat down among that accursed crew but that he should come through it without breaking. But he broke then."

He got up abruptly and walked over to the window. For a while he stood there, looking out into the August twilight. Then he turned. The other two had not stirred.

"However, Alberic had over-reached himself at last. Palestrina's own voice was shaking, when he gave the benediction and dissolved the Council. I saw Abelard for a moment, before Geoffrey of St. Médard took him. Then I waited to try to see Palestrina alone, but the others were glued to him. I rode as far as Vierzy last night. To-night I must see the Bishop here—you will help me there, Gilles. And tomorrow, I must ride on to Sens."

Gilles sat silent, looking straight before him.

"They will do what they will do," he said at last, in a strange toneless voice. "But I know this. I shall not live to see it, nor you, Geoffrey, nor even Pierre maybe. But when this generation is dead, the youngsters in Paris will be reading his books, though some other name will be upon them, and they will be taught by the men that Abelard taught to think, though they will not name his name. And some day, it may be a hundred years from now, it may be two hundred, but some man will speak again of reason and authority, as he did, and will bring together the whole *Summa* of theology by just such methods as his, and they will write that man's name in the Calendar of Saints and they will handle his book as if it were the Ark of the Covenant. But meantime they will have hounded Abelard to death."

After a long silence, Geoffrey spoke.

"*Except a grain of wheat fall into the ground and die, it abideth alone. But if it die—*"

Pierre de Montboissier had sprung to his feet.

"You know nothing about him," he cried. "He was never your master," and with that he went hurriedly from the room.

CHAPTER II

THIBAULT was fishing. Just below the rocky hillock where he and Master Peter had built their huts and their thatched oratory, the Arduzon made a great pool. Honeysuckle and alders hung over it, giving good cover to the fisherman, and great boulders lay in the pool, giving good cover to the trout. There was no sunlight, this first of November, but there was a glow in the air, a diffused reflection from the oaks and beeches of the forest that stood up like golden fountains, and the brambles that burnt along the ground like creeping fire. Thibault's heart was light, and as he listened to the faint clink of a chisel on stone from the hill above him, he blessed God and his uncle Thibault of Champagne, who had given Master Peter this place.

For Thibault himself, he asked nothing better than that they should live here for ever, they two, until they died. Master Peter, it seemed to him, had braved the world long enough, and the world had very nearly broken him. There was that damnable trial for heresy, to begin with. And though Ralph of Rheims got red in the face when it was spoken of, and it was only a few weeks till Palestrina had him released from the penitentiary and returned to St. Denis, it had done something to his master. He was different. Thibault used to be a sound sleeper, though not so sound as before that night—Thibault crossed himself: he had asked old Herluin at Coincy to say a Mass on All Souls for poor Guibert—but now night after night he wakened with Master Peter crying out in his sleep, shouting sometimes that he was no heretic, arguing interminably with someone he called Gosvin, or, worst of all, moaning to himself. Once he had cried out, a terrible bitter cry—"Christ, where wert Thou?" in a voice like the cry from the Cross. But in the daytime he was very gentle, only given to long fits of brooding.

And then there was the trouble at St. Denis, whatever it was, some argument that Thibault never rightly got to the bottom of, about whether St. Denis was Dionysius the Areopagite or not, and whether the Venerable Bede who said he was not was more to be believed in than the Abbot Hilduin who said he was, and had gone to Greece to make sure. As a Frenchman, Thibault inclined to the Abbot Hilduin, as against the Englishman: but if Master Peter preferred Bede, he was right: and he could not see why the Abbot Adam had made such a pother about it, talked even of treason and of handing him over to the King's justice for miscalling the patron saint of France. Abbot Adam would have liked to see Master Peter broken on the wheel, like enough. It was a January

night, Thibault remembered, when he waited with two
horses below the wall at St. Denis, and some decent
brother inside let Master Peter down by a rope, and they
had ridden down to Provins together, and Master Peter
had been taken in by the brethren at St. Ayoul. And then,
though Count Thibault had done what he could, Abbot
Adam very nearly had him back again. They would have
beaten him to death, thought Thibault, or starved him to
death: he was only a handful of bones when he took him
in his arms from the rope that night. It was God's mercy
that let fly a stroke on Abbot Adam, after too hearty a
meal, and with a good deal of to-do Suger, the new
Abbot, had consented to set Master Peter free, on condition that he went to no other abbey. It seemed odd,
thought Thibault, that they could neither live with him
nor without him. But anyhow they were determined that
nobody else should make a boast of having him.

At any rate, he was free for ever and ever of St. Denis.
Thibault's uncle had wanted to make him his chaplain:
it was a sin, he said, that a man with an eye for a hawk
like his should ever have been a monk: and when Master
Peter had reminded him in plain terms of the bar to his
ordination, Thibault had got red in the face and said it
was a queer thing they'd ordain a goose-brained block
like his nephew, and swore that Master Peter should have
his pick of Champagne, and found an abbey of his own,
if he liked. And when he had chosen the little tongue of
ground at the edge of the forest, almost an island with
the tiny reach of the river that looped round it, though
in a dry summer it was only a gravel-bed with a few
pools, Thibault had given it to him in perpetuity.

"I'll be none the worse," said he, "of a holy hermit on

my doorstep to say an odd prayer for me now and again."

That was what they would be, Thibault thought. Master Peter would live here, like St. Jerome in his cave, and he would be the lion that brought home the wood. In a year's time he would be old enough to be ordained, and could say Mass in the oratory, instead of their having to walk to Coincy: for his master had an odd shrinking from strangers. Master Peter would read and write, while he swept the floor and baked the bread and fished and hoed the plot that he must soon fence in to keep the hens from scrabbling in it. They had done well, the sitting he had got from Hugh the Forester's wife, though it was full late in the year. He would have half a dozen pullets out of them, and a cockerel or two, that he would kill for Martinmas, and another for Christmas. Thibault frowned a little, thinking of the winter. Master Peter was always better when he could be out and about, and doing something with his hands.

He had never been so well as when they were building their huts. They had brought the reeds from the reed bed down the Arduzon, near St. Pierre de Boissenay. Thibault had been surprised to see how handy Master Peter had been with the thatching, but he said he used to help Goose-Foot the Thatcher when he was a youngster in Brittany: and he had spent hours making a pattern in the thatch along the eaves of the oratory, while Thibault daubed the walls with mud to make them wind-proof. They would be busy for another while digging the ground for the spring sowing, though Master Peter had small strength for the digging, but came patiently after, crumbling the clods, and throwing lame Thomas the worms. But when the rain and the frost would come,

and they could do little but sit and look at one another
over the fire? For Master Peter read little these days. He
would take out his books, but Thibault saw him sit hour
after hour and never turn a page. And he wrote not at all.
However, Thibault was determined that he would make
a search that day when he went back to his father's at
Provins. He remembered a chest full of old parchments
with the ink very faint. Parchment was dear, but if he
had some pumice stone and scraped them, Master Peter
could write on these. He would be happy, if only he
would begin to write. Meantime, the figure he was making in stone of the Holy Trinity, to put above the altar in
their oratory, would keep him busy for a long while.
Thibault calculated it, contentedly.

Three trout: that must do, though he would like to
have waited for the great fellow under the stone. He
had seen him there. They had seen each other, that was
the worst of it. Thibault sighed: he could have sat all
day watching the slim, gray ghosts flit through the pale
water. It was a better day than yesterday: there had been
too much sun. He wound up his line, cleaned his three
trout with an expert finger, and threw the guts to
Thomas, the lame duck that he had brought up himself,
ever since the clumsy hen who had hatched them out
stood on him and crushed his leg. Thomas walked behind Thibault everywhere, sitting with his yellow eye
fixed on him as he thatched or dug, and now followed
every movement of the rod as intelligently as Thibault
himself. Thomas had nothing to do with his brethren,
now peacefully asleep on the further bank, their bills
reversed on their backs. Queer, thought Thibault, how
they sleep in the middle of the morning: but then, they

are early risers and late walkers. Thomas unluckily made noises of gratification over his meal; in a trice every head came undone and the whole fleet were paddling across the river and falling over one another up the bank. With a frightful effort Thomas spooned up the last fragment and stood, blinking but triumphant. Thibault stooped to pick him up, and climbed up the track. Odd, he thought, as the indignant quacking died behind him to a soft gabble, that Master Peter should dislike the sound so. It seemed to Thibault one of the pleasantest noises in the world. However, though he had not liked the idea of their having ducks, he had grown fond of them when they first came out, would sit for long enough watching their solemn antics. And to Thomas he had become as attached as Thibault himself.

The clink of the chisel had been silent for some time, Thibault realized uncomfortably. However, his foot snapped a twig as he came up the track, and it began again. As he came through the hazel copse into the clearing, Abelard was working with an air of great cheerfulness at a fold of God the Father's cloak.

"What do you think of it, Thibault?" said he, stepping back. "You see, the cloak is to fall over both their shoulders, the Son on one side, and the Holy Ghost on the other."

"There'll be nothing better at Chartres," affirmed Thibault, regardless that the faces of the Trinity were still blank masses of stone. "I'll be curious to see the Holy Ghost. I've never seen a likeness of him to my knowledge, unless as a kind of a bird, like."

Thomas wriggled, and flopped unwieldly to the ground. A gleam came into Abelard's eye.

[249]

"We'll not ask Thomas to sit, anyhow," said he.

The joke, and above all the fact that Master Peter was again making a joke, enchanted Thibault. He bellowed with laughter, and Master Peter joined in, the more at the stony stare which Thomas fixed upon them.

"Look here, Thibault," said he, "that fowl of yours is getting too serious. It's exactly the Blessed Gosvin's eye, when I used to make a joke in the old days at St. Geneviève."

"Thank God he's greedy," said Thibault. "He nearly burst himself getting the last of the trout guts down before the others could reach him. Three trout. I thought they'd do for our suppers."

"If I don't eat them all for my dinner," said Master Peter. "You'll have been fed so full at Provins that you'll have room for nothing when you get back. It's time you were away, lad. Where are you to meet Hugh with the pony?"

"He said he was coming to Mass at Coincy," said Thibault. "I'm walking that length. I said I'd serve Mass for old Herluin." He hesitated. "And, sir, I was to tell you he would be proud if he might give you your dinner."

Abelard was silent for a moment. "I think I'll let you do duty for the two of us, Thibault," he said, with seeming lightness. "I'll go down tomorrow. All Souls are more my line of country than All Saints."

Thibault's face fell. But it was not for him to preach attendance at the sacraments to his god. Besides, he might have known that he would shirk dinner with old Herluin.

"I'll be getting away, then," he said. "You'll cook yourself the trout, won't you?"

"I'll cook myself something," said Abelard. "But I lost

[250]

the last trout I cooked in the fire. It fell off the stick."

"Well, there's two eggs," said Thibault. "And I'll cook the trout myself when I get back this evening."

"Take my cloak off the bed," said Abelard. "It's warmer than yours. There'll be a frost tonight."

Thibault stooped his head under the low thatch, and came out with it over his arm. "I'm going to ask a calf-skin from my father," said he, "to make us a pair of boots apiece for the winter."

"You'll ask your father for nothing, Thibault, do you hear?" said Abelard, suddenly flushing. "I was shamed to my soul the last time you came home. If I can't dig, at least I won't beg."

Thibault looked at him obstinately. "I'll beg none," said he. "But I'm going to ask him for a calf-skin to make us boots, and a barrel of salt herrings against the time the water gets frozen. I cost him a deal more in one week in Paris, I can tell you, than anything I get from him now. And sure the old man might as well make his soul this way as any other."

Abelard opened his mouth to fiery rejoinder, and shut it again. The look of dumb patience on his face all but broke Thibault's heart.

"I'll ask him for nothing, Master Peter," said he. "But if he chooses to give me this and that, you wouldn't have me refuse my own father?"

"I don't know why you stay with me, Thibault," said Abelard. "But I'd starve in a week if you didn't. There, lad, get along with you." He forced himself to smile and turned back with a great show of industry to his stone. "And, Thibault," he said, but without looking round,

"make my excuses to Herluin, and thank him kindly for
his hospitality."

Thibault looked at him for a moment with sorrowful
eyes, and disappeared down the track to the river.
Thomas walked after him a step or two, but realizing
that the pace was beyond him, came back and sat by the
god of his god.

"And I couldn't even send the boy away happy for his
one holiday," thought Abelard. "But to be thankful for
the offer of a dinner from a little prying, drunken priest.
And live on the charity of peasants that think I'm a kind
of a wizard, and that fat oaf, Thibault's father. And none
of them sure that I'm not a heretic." He dropped the
chisel on the grass and stood up. He must not let himself think.

Yet what was a man to do in this wilderness but think?
He gazed around him, and in spite of himself the tiny
dwelling-places that he and Thibault had made, looked
at him reproachfully. They were like the little houses
that he and Guillaume and Raoul used to build in the
valley where the hazel trees grew. He twitched his mind
away. Was there any one channel down which it could
run, now that half his life was shut off from him, and half
the chambers of his brain bolted and shuttered and dark,
only that his thoughts at night fluttered in them like bats?
Gilles said she was prioress now. Some day perhaps, when
she was an old woman, they might see one another again.
But now, at the mere sight of her handwriting his heart
turned over. Last year they had brought the mortuary
roll of St. Vitalis to St. Denis, for the brethren to inscribe
their sympathy with the bereaved house. The roll had
come to St. Denis from Argenteuil: someone at Argen-

[252]

teuil had written half a dozen lines on death. It was not
signed, but it was in her script. It had been several nights
before he had quiet sleep. Some day she would cease to
haunt him. Some day he would be able to think of her as
God's bride, who had been his wild love in just such
woods as these. But what was the desire of the flesh beside the desire of the mind?

He looked about him in despair. Under the beeches
the brown hens walked and scuffled, flicking the yellow
and russet leaves this way and that, absorbed and happy:
from the pool below came the flat, contented voices of
the ducks. He took his staff, and flung into the woods.

As he walked, the tumult in his brain died, leaving
the dull, familiar ache. It was almost easier, after all, he
thought, to bear the sudden resurrection of remembrance,
than this grief without a ripple, without ebb or flow, a
kind of dark water that lay sullen at his heart root. For
a while in St. Médard he had almost gone mad. He had
been so utterly confident, so sure of God: and God had
forsaken him, had gone over to the side of Alberic and
Ralph and Palestrina; of jealousy and stupidity and hypocrisy. They had tricked and cheated and lied, and
they had won. They had destroyed his book that had
been his burnt-offering to God, the symbol that he was
now and for ever Christ's philosopher. They had destroyed his book and Alberic was Abel, and God had had
respect to his offering, and he was the branded Cain.

Walking heedlessly but rapidly, he had covered more
ground than he knew; it was with a shock of surprise
that he found himself where the trees thinned on the hill
above the valley where Coincy lay. Like a wild duck's
nest, he thought, looking down at it, and his heart

softened at the patches of the fields, the tiny roofs. He
could have sat there long enough, blessing them, as he
had sat watching the antics of Thibault's yellow duck-
lings, so small, so eager to live, so pitifully easy to crush.
But even as he stood watching, brooding over them in a
grim, thwarted tenderness, a small sound came to his ears,
high and thin almost as a gnat's voice. The tiny bell on
the church had begun to ring, summoning these tiny
souls, hedgers and ditchers and shambling old men and
women with child, to sit down with Apostles and Martyrs, St. Ambrose and St. Augustine and the unnumbered
manes of the unnamed holy dead. And listening, a great
longing took him to go in and sit among them: to feel
no more the outcast, the man whom God had rejected
and would have no longer to serve Him. It might be
that the miracle would happen, that he might receive the
Host without such a spring of bitterness in his heart as
turned the sacrament to poison.

The village seemed empty as he passed through it:
every soul must be in church. He reached the graveyard
and passed up the uneven stones to the low door. But
there a queer reluctance seized him: he sat down on the
stone ledge of the porch to take breathing space, and
courage to go in. The Alleluia was just ending: there
was a pause, and Herluin's hoarse relaxed voice began the
Gospel, reading aloud the Beatitudes that are for broken
men, for men that are poor in spirit, for men that mourn,
for men that hunger and thirst after righteousness, for
men that are reviled and all manner of evil spoken against
them falsely. *Rejoice and be exceeding glad, for great is
your reward in heaven.* Well, he was broken enough, he
had mourned, he had hungered and thirsted after right-

[254]

eousness, at any rate after truth, there had been evil enough said of him. But he was not blessed. There were some that God rejected, and He had rejected him.

Then fell a silence, then Thibault's young voice, the boys' voices following it. "*The souls of the just are in the hand of God, and the torment of malice shall not touch them: in the sight of the unwise they seemed to die, but they are in peace.*"

He rose and went quietly out of the porch and past the quiet graves. The torment of malice had touched him: the hand of God was not for him. The whole gentleness of the November day, the day that seemed to him more than any other to have Good Friday's peace, dreamt above the world, but not on him. He had no anger now, no bitterness even. He had blasphemed God once, but he blasphemed no more. "*Though He slay me, yet will I trust in Him*"—why did they never finish that sentence as Job finished it?—"*but I will maintain my ways before Him. . . . My righteousness I hold fast, and I will not let it go.*"

He halted suddenly, for in this queer silence of the earth, with all the saints intent upon the prayers of the faithful, and all the world droning with devotion like a hive of bees, now if ever it seemed to him that he might speak and God would hear, with only the two of them left face to face. He stood quiet and grim, his face turned to the quiet sky. All the traditions of his faith, all the memories of his life were forcing him upon his knees, but he would not. His mother's silent abnegation, the humility of his father's walk with God, the whole divine consolation of psalmist and prophet pleaded with him in vain. "*As far as east is distant from the west, so far hath He removed our*

transgressions from us." Let him first be shown wherein
he had transgressed. "*Like as a father pitieth his children,
so the Lord pitieth them that fear Him.*" He asked for
no pity, he asked for justice, the justice that a man would
give his fellow, aye, that a lord would give his serf.

And standing there, braced against heaven, the wind
that had blown upon him once and been forgotten,
breathed upon him again. It came without observation,
for the kingdom of God is within: a frail wisp of
memory, voiceless as the drift of thistle-down, inevitable
as sunrise. "*Neither do I condemn thee: go, and sin no
more.*"

He saw no heavens opened: he saw no Son of Man.
For a moment it seemed to him that all the vital forces
in his body were withdrawing themselves, that the sight
had left his eyes and the blood was ebbing from his
heart: he felt the gray breath of dissolution, the falling
asunder of body and soul. For a moment: then his spirit
leapt toward heaven in naked adoration. Stripped of all
human emotion, with no warmth of contrition, with no
passion of devotion, but with every power of his mind,
with every pulse of his body, he worshiped God.

Hours later, he found himself on the edge of the forest
where the road came up from the ford and passed over
the hill to Rigny-la-Vanneuse. Instinctively he had left
the river for the hills, and had walked mile after mile,
skirting the woods, keeping the valley below him. Yet it
was no blind ecstasy that had driven him so far: his brain
had never worked with so steady a rhythm. It was not
so much that the first glory had passed as that it had
transmuted itself into a grave clarity: and halting now

[256]

at the boundary stone, he turned and looked back along the valley, its small, green meadows by the river and the patches of plowed earth, torn open to be softened by frost and rain. The mist had cleared, and though the sky was still veiled, the veil was translucent.

" '*And now men see not the brightness in the clouds,*' " said Abelard to himself, " '*but the wind passeth and cleanseth them.*' "

It had been so with him. In the long hours of his ceaseless walking, ceaseless thinking, he had been aware of no conscious examining of himself. But as in that definition Gilles had quoted to him of infinity, the years of his intellectual majority had seemed present to him in a single moment of time, with all their implications, the shadows that they cast before and after, above all the years since he had turned his back on the world and as he had thought, sought the Kingdom of God. Every sentence he had written stood out before him, that glorious array of embattled spears, his strong chivalry of all the powers of the soul, of all the strength of the mind, pagan and Christian; Plato and Aristotle fighting side by side with Augustine and Jerome and Origen, for the conquest of the spirit's Palestine, for the worship of the Father in spirit and in truth. But for whom was the glory of that warfare? He had fought against ignorance, against hypocrisy, against spiritual sloth, against an easy faith that was the faith of gulls and not of men: he had written for his young men, challenging them to doubt, arming them against the deadlier sin of dullness: but did dullness keep a man more insensitive to God than pride?

"If a man desire to understand God, let him prepare himself for that understanding by good life and let him take the way of humility, for by that road alone may a man come nigh that height of intellectual vision." It sounded reverent enough, but how his heart had swelled as he had written it, in a kind of pomp of abnegation: the pride of that humility was the ceremonial pride of the Roman salute. He had strutted like a beadle in a cathedral procession, forgetting that behind him came the Host.

"I have heard of thee by the hearing of the ear, but now mine eye seeth thee: wherefore I do abhor myself." This very day he had challenged Heaven to show him wherein he had sinned: and Heaven's answer had been to show him itself. His righteousness he had held fast and would not let it go: it lay about him now, like farmyard-trampled snow.

And now? He stood looking down at the river as it flowed through the quiet land. And something in the still, shining surface of it brought back to him a thing that he had forgotten for more than thirty years. Once when he was a youngster he had gone with his father on pilgrimage to St. Gildas de Rhuis. It was a quiet, shining day with no wind, and standing on those terrible cliffs above the point and looking westward, he had seen a strange silver pathway that swept round the headland and out to sea, with no ripple upon it, counter to all the restless fleeing and pursuing of the blue gay-crested waves. His father had stood beside him, so withdrawn into himself that for a long time he had not liked to question him: and when he did, Berengar had answered heavily, with his eyes still upon it, "It is the will of God." At supper in the guest-house, the old brother who waited on them spoke of the strong current that swept round the coast and was the terror of all craft that made for home: and

[258]

yet it had suffered St. Gildas to float upon it without oar or sail, and landed him unbroken in his coracle in the cove where his image stood. He saw it now, looking down into the valley, as though the river had transformed itself into that swift current, radiant, implacable and strong, and the green fields into the jabble of the tumbling waves. Well, it had brought his father to a quiet haven: it was to take himself to sea.

A shudder of premonition passed over him. To what end would it carry him, St. Brendan's Happy Isles, or the sea, shouting on an iron coast? Through what sore discipline of body and soul, through what crucifixion of his pride must he still go, before he saw the Kingdom of God? For a moment his flesh and his heart failed. Then he raised his head and began walking steadily towards home. He was chanting as he walked, the words that had held for him the torment of all longing and now were for ever his. "*The souls of the just are in the hand of God, and the torment of malice shall not touch them; in the sight of the unwise they seemed to die, but they are in peace.*" He had turned to the stronghold of the prisoners of hope.

It was almost sunset when he dropped down into the Arduzon valley, and took the track by the river that led home. The touch of frost that he had promised Thibault was in the air, and he quickened his pace, for he must have the fire lit and some comfort for the boy after his long ride. He would come laden, Abelard well knew, and half shy of showing his spoils, after his sharpness of the morning. He must make amends for that, make much of everything, praise the calf-skin and exult in the little barrel of salted herrings: but if he did not hurry, all the excitement of the arrival would be spoiled: Thibault would find the huts deserted and no fire to welcome him. The last glow was on the trunks of the trees as he came through the hazel copse into the clearing, and again something stirred in his heart, as it had that morning five years ago in Brittany when he reined in on the hillside and looked to Le Palais. So forlorn they were, the little houses with their heavy thatch and low doorways: they had done their best, God knew, to comfort him, and he would have none of them. He looked at them, smiling, and blessed them: then the smile broadened, for he saw the hens sitting reproachfully before their door, that he had shut in absence of mind the last time he went in for firewood. They roused with a drowsy chunnering as he went through them to open it, and lumbered sleepily after him: a couple made off round the house with the air of being awake and up for the rest of the night, but a few grains flung inside the smelly little house brought them in, and he closed the door, listening to the soft whirr of wings as one by one they took the short flight to the roost. Thomas at sight of him had risen and walked into their own hut: he would have composed himself by now on Thibault's bed. He could hear the voices of the ducks still down on the river, but they were always late to bed. Time enough to bring them up when he had kindled the fire. Oh, lovely twilight ghost! He knelt a moment on the threshold of the oratory, crying her name towards the dim altar, and came away.

The fire was not long in kindling: the hearthplace was still warm. He blew it for a while so that he might have red embers instead of green wood for the grilling of Thibault's trout, and then went out to gather chestnuts and set them roasting on the stones that banked in the fire. Thomas sat on the skin that covered Thibault's bed and observed him. He was just placing the last chestnut when he heard the bridle ring and went out into the dusk. He could hear a hoof pawing soft ground and the pony blowing through its nostrils with an impatient shake of the bit, but there was no sign of Thibault. He went through the hazel copse and looked down. There was the stocky pony halted in the hollow, and Thibault in frantic haste unroping a bundle and stowing it under a clump of furze.

"Greedy gut," said Abelard. "Making a private larder for yourself, are you?"

Thibault looked up aghast.

"If I was a mule this morning, you're a donkey now," said Abelard. "Bring it out of that, man, and I'll bring up the pony." He came down and took the little creature by the head and up the steep track, Thibault, bewildered and enchanted, coming after.

"I tell you," said Abelard, "the pony deserves its supper, if it carried that load and yourself all the way from Provins. How ever did you manage it?"

"I walked," said Thibault. "And honestly, Master Peter, I asked my father for not one thing but a few old parchments he has there in a chest. But my mother had been looking out this and that for weeks, and it was all piled in the loft ready. And she would have me take whatever was left of our dinner, so we needn't roast the trout. There's a couple of roast duck, and marchpane, and, Sir, you will not be angry, but my father sends you a little tonneau of wine and asks your blessing. And my mother has sent us sheepskins to line our coats for the winter and a bearskin for your bed—I'll leave it over the pony, for he's hot—we came quick at the last. And a cheese. And by the next time I go my father says he will have a goat for us, but most of them are not milking now."

"Well, I've been busy myself," said Abelard. "You never saw that I've been roasting your chestnuts."

Thibault's eyes were the eyes of a dog, intolerable with affection.

"I hear a lot of talk," went on Abelard righteously, "about wine and marchpane and ducks, but that's all I see of them. I suppose you are as tight as a drum, but my two sides are clapped in. I'm so hungry I'm a pain to myself."

Thibault, on his knees unpacking, stopped and looked up at the shelf.

"Did you never find the eggs?"

"I went for a long walk," said Abelard, "longer than I meant. And I am just this moment back, afraid I would get my head in my hands for letting the fire out." He seized the cheese that had rolled under Thibault's arm, and cut a half-moon out of it. "It should by rights come last," he said, "but I can bear myself no longer. Now get out your fowls, Thibault. Both of them. And did you say wine?"

Thibault was too happy for speech. He was busy un-roping the little barrel, and Abelard had risen, the segment of cheese in his hand, to reach down their drinking-horns from the wall, when both men suddenly stood still.

"My God," said Thibault, "what's that?"

From somewhere near them in the woods a cry had risen, a thin cry, of such intolerable anguish that Abelard turned dizzy on his feet, and caught at the wall.

"It's a child's voice," he said. "O God, are they at a child?"

Thibault had gone outside. The cry came again, making the twilight and the firelit hearth a mockery.

"A rabbit," said Thibault. He listened. "There's nothing worrying it. It'll be in a trap. Hugh told me he was putting them down. Christ!" The scream came yet again.

Abelard was beside him, and the two plunged down the bank.

"Down by the river," said Thibault. "I saw them playing, God help them, when I was coming home. You know the way they go demented with fun in the evenings. It will have been drumming with its hind paws to itself and brought down the trap."

Abelard went on, hardly listening. "Oh, God," he was muttering. "Let it die. Let it die quickly."

But the cry came yet again. On the right, this time. He plunged through a thicket of hornbeam.

"Watch out," said Thibault, thrusting past him. "The trap might take the hand off you."

The rabbit stopped shrieking when they stooped over it, either from exhaustion, or in some last extremity of fear. Thibault held the teeth of the trap apart, and Abelard gathered up the little creature in his hands. It lay for a moment breathing quickly, then in some blind recognition of the kindness that had met it at the last, the small head thrust and nestled against his arm, and it died.

It was that last confiding thrust that broke Abelard's heart. He looked down at the little draggled body, his mouth shaking. "Thibault," he said, "do you think there is a God at all? Whatever has come to me, I earned it. But what did this one do?"

Thibault nodded.

"I know," he said. "Only—I think God is in it too."

Abelard looked up sharply.

"In it? Do you mean that it makes Him suffer, the way it does us?"

Again Thibault nodded.

"Then why doesn't He stop it?"

"I don't know," said Thibault. "Unless—unless it's like the Prodigal Son. I suppose the father could have kept him at home against his will. But what would have been the use? All this," he stroked the limp body, "is because of us. But all the time God suffers. More than we do."

Abelard looked at him, perplexed.

"Thibault, when did you think of all this?"

Thibault's face stiffened. "It was that night," he said, his voice strangled. "The things we did to—to poor Guibert. He—" Thibault stopped. "I could not sleep for nights and nights. And then I saw that God suffered too. And I thought I would like to be a priest."

"Thibault, do you mean Calvary?"

Thibault shook his head. "That was only a piece of it —the piece that we saw—in time. Like that." He pointed to a fallen tree beside them, sawn through the middle. "That dark ring there, it goes up and down the whole length of the tree. But you only see it where it is cut across. That is what Christ's life was; the bit of God that we saw. And we think God is like that, because Christ was like that, kind, and forgiving sins and healing people. We think God is like that for ever, because it happened once, with Christ. But not the pain. Not the agony at the last. We think that stopped."

Abelard looked at him, the blunt nose and the wide mouth, the honest troubled eyes. He could have knelt before him.

"Then, Thibault," he said slowly, "you think that all this," he looked down at the little quiet body in his arms, "all the pain of the world, was Christ's cross?"

"God's cross," said Thibault. "And it goes on."

"The Patripassian heresy," muttered Abelard mechanically. "But, oh, God, if it were true. Thibault, it must be. At least, there is something at the back of it that is true. And if we could find it—it would bring back the whole world."

"I couldn't ever rightly explain it," said Thibault. "But you could, if you would think it out." He reached out his hand, and stroked the long ears. "Old lop-ears," he said. "Maybe this is why he died. Come and have your supper, Master Peter. We'll bury him somewhere near the oratory. In holy ground."

CHAPTER III

MEN's sins were forgiven them, long before the Passion: Mary Magdalene, for instance, and the paralytic, to whom Our Lord said, 'Son, thy sins be forgiven thee.' What necessity, what reason, what need was there for the Son of God to endure such intolerable anguish, when the divine compassion was able to deliver a man from the evil one, by the sole vision of Himself? When it seems to us both cruel and unjust to

[265]

demand the blood of the innocent in any kind of bargain, or to find any kind of pleasure that the innocent should be slain, how should God find the death of His Son so agreeable, that thereby He should be reconciled to the world? These, and other thoughts like them, seem to me to raise no small question as to our redemption by the death of Our Lord."

Gilles groaned aloud. "First the Trinity," he muttered to himself, "and now the Atonement. That man was born to trouble, as the sparks fly upward." He laid down Abelard's close-written sheet on his knee, and his eye traveled to the window. The sun was still low in the east: why, wondered Gilles, should this level light transfigure the earth, beyond any magic of sunrise or sunset? He saw the bare trees of the Terrain beyond the eastern wall of the cloister, the swift gray current of the Seine, and across the narrow strait the Ile Notre Dame with its black piles of wood and turf, the grass between them a strange passionate green. There is more color, he thought, in November than there is in August, except perhaps in water. The river knows it may be frozen in a week, and it runs ice-gray already. For water dies: the earth never. Those naked trees, indifferent to the fall of the leaf: the life is more than meat, they say, and the body than raiment: what we have we hold. Perhaps, thought Gilles, it was because he himself was in his November, and the last day of it too, he added with a crooked smile, that the autumn seemed to him richer than any spring, and this pale persistent sunlight had a kind of heroic tenderness. There is no memory in spring, he thought, not even the memory of other springs: but a November day of faint sunlight and emerald moss remembers all things, the

[266]

wild promise of the January days, snow-broth in February, violets in March, new-mown hay in June, dew-wet mint trodden underfoot on August nights, the harvest moon in September, the hunter's moon in October. Prudentius, he thought, was the November of the poets: Prudentius remembering

> "How many times the rose
> Returned after the snows."

No other poet in the world had that still clarity. It had baffled him always; he could find no metaphor that did not do violence to it, that quality neither of dawn nor noonday nor sunset. He had it now: it was this level light, of the sun near the horizon.

Sixty, when he began to write poetry, and entered the Kingdom of God. Ausonius, too, wrote his best poetry at seventy, after Paulinus broke his heart. It seems, thought Gilles ruefully, to be the condition of eternal life, for saints or for poets. For himself, he had no heart to break: but such as he had, had very nearly broken for this man whose letter lay on his lap: and for the woman whom he was to see that day. Queer, thought Gilles, that one could go through life, tasting it, chewing the sweet and spitting out the bitter, living with one's stomach and one's brain: and when one might reasonably think all heat of the blood and folly of impulse were past, to have the heart torn out of your breast for two creatures nearly half a century away.

She was coming to fetch Denise's two girls: they were to be novices at Argenteuil. Their uncle Raoul, the canon of Nantes, had brought them last night, and had them out with him now to show them Paris. Agatha and Agnes:

they were like fawns, Heloise had said, trembling on the edge of a wood: like fawns still, Gilles thought, remembering them hand in hand at the foot of his bed that morning. Though Agatha, when he asked her a question about her reading, had raised her head and gazed straight at him, and with a shock he had found himself looking into Abelard's eyes. That a man's ghost should walk in his own life-time. She was far liker him than his brother Raoul, a stocky comfortable little man. Well, it was easily seen that they worshiped Heloise. Their aunt, they called her. Odd how one jibbed at hearing the ordinary human relations applied to a spirit like hers. Yet once, even to himself, she had been no more than Fulbert's niece.

At that memory, it seemed to Gilles that he opened a door into an empty house that had been firelit once, and now was naked rafters under the sky. He was living comfortably enough, they said, on one of his farms, with old Grizzel to tend him: his mind gone. Gilles paused a moment to think that life is sadder than any graveyard: that a man is his own burial-place. Queer, queer, to see what can befall a man when he is old. Shipwreck in youth is sorrowful enough, but one looks for storms at the spring equinox. Yet it is the September equinox that drowns. A comfortable doctrine, the perseverance of the saints: a pity that so few of the comfortable doctrines were true.

So at any rate Abelard seemed to think: the comfortable doctrine of the ransom, for instance, and the debt paid once for all. Gilles returned to the neglected sheet upon his knee. "What then is our redemption? We are justified in the blood of Christ and reconciled to God, because by the life and death of His Son He has so bound

[268]

us to Himself that love so kindled will shrink from nothing for His sake. Our redemption is that supreme devotion kindled in us by the Passion of Christ: this it is that
frees us from the slavery of sin and gives us the liberty
of the sons of God, so that we do His will from love and
not from fear. This is that fire which Our Lord said He
had come to kindle upon earth." He has never written
like this, thought Gilles; his words are like burning coals.
"It is the goodness of God that leads us to repentance:
we grieve to have sinned against God, from love, and
not from fear, less because He is just than because He is
merciful. We are reconciled to God in that grief: in
whatsoever hour the sinner shall grieve, says Ezekiel, he
shall be saved: that is, he is made fit to be saved."

Gilles stroked his chin reflectively. "It is no easy way
of holiness," he thought to himself. "Not saved, but only
made fit to be saved. Now, if that had been preached to
me in my youth? It is no wonder that he has emptied
Paris. Well, Jehan?"

Jehan's tawny head had come round the door. "The
young mistress is below. Am I to bring her up?"

Gilles's hands shook. "Set a chair for her. Have you the
wine cooling?"

"Aye."

"The Moselle?"

"Aye. Will I bring her some marchpane?"

"No. But a fresh loaf with a good crust on it. You
might know better by this time than to affront a good
wine with sweet stuff."

Jehan grunted and the door shut. Gilles thrust the
letter under the skin that lay across his bed. Perhaps he

need never show it to her, but speak as if Thibault had only brought him word of mouth. For there was still no letter for her: and in this letter no message. Gilles divined the reason. There are some things a man must let be, till he has strength to handle them. But how could she, being a woman, know? That was her foot on the stair, and he was as short of breath as if he had climbed a hill. He heard her come into the room where he had always received her, and pause a little. God help her, it was not his ghost she would see there, but another. Then the door opened, and his heart ceased shaking through him and was quiet. His day had flowered.

She stood for a moment without moving, looking at him, and it seemed to him that some spring of mercy in her overflowed and steeped his heart in its strange dew. Laughter used to well in her, he remembered, and the light come and go on her face like the broken lights of running water. It was a still face now: the line from the wings of the nose to the side of the mouth should never have been graven so deep. He had seen it graven in a year, the line that comes from a mouth set not to cry. Thank God, it was less deep now than it had been. But the eyes—it was the eyes that opened the gates of mercy on mankind.

She sighed, a little contented sigh.

"To see you again," she said, and without moving at all, it seemed to him, she was beside him, lifting his hands to her mouth.

"And very handsome you are in bed," she went on, creasing her eyes at him.

"I had Jehan shaving me for you at six," said Gilles complacently.

"But, Gilles, should you be sitting up? Jehan says your sciatica is cruel."

"I shall die sitting up," said Gilles. "I will not have him pour my soup over my face as if he were manuring rhubarb. I had two days of it. But I made him haul me up this morning. Did you read your Psalms for the day, Heloise? 'Thou knowest my downsitting and mine uprising'? It might well be, for I bellowed like a bull. Jehan there can tell you. Bring the wine here, Jehan. Is it cold enough?"

Jehan grunted, but decanted it carefully enough into a wrought green cup of forest glass.

"Where's my own cup?" said Gilles.

"Master Simon said you was to drink none," said Jehan doggedly.

"What?" exploded Gilles. "Tell Master Simon I'm not Dives in Hell yet," he went on, controlling himself. "And tell him that I had sciatica and drank myself out of it when he was cutting his first tooth. I am surprised you heeded him, Jehan. That's better. That will do."

Jehan went out.

"Drink, Heloise."

She lifted the cup slowly to her lips. "It is a strange wine," she said. "It is cold and green like well-water, a forest well: and when you drink it, it warms you like a fire, no, more like the molten sun."

"That was why I chose it for you," said Gilles. "I have always drunk it, since I knew you, naming your name."

She turned her eyes on him, accepting him.

"Where does it come from?"

"Moselle. Is it not a strange thing that a man with a palate like Ausonius should have written a long poem describing every fin on every fish in that dull river, and not a word in all its four hundred and eighty-three hexameters about the vineyards? Maybe, as a Bordeaux man, he thought little of them. Yet a man's palate should have no *patria*."

"Are you sure, Gilles? I think you used to quote me a lovely line, about a vine. *Tremit . . . tremit—*"

"What did I tell you? *'Tremit absens!'*

> "Trembles the absent vine and swells the grape
> In thy clear crystal."

Heloise sighed again, in pure content. She sat, holding up the great cup in her two hands, her eyes on the quick gray river. Something had brought a trouble to them.

"Is it true," said Gilles abruptly, "that my cousin is drinking herself to death?"

Heloise's eyes came back to his face.

"She is."

"She had my palate," said Gilles. "Well, we are hard to kill. I give her two years. You will be the next Abbess."

Heloise shook her head.

"Why not? Do not tell me it will be another case of St. Anselm and the crozier and the *Nolo episcopari?*"

"No," said Heloise quietly. "I can do the work. They made me Prioress. They might as well make me Abbess. If one's heart is utterly hollow, no one seems to notice any difference. Is it St. James or Ecclesiastes?—'Whatsoever thy hand findeth to do, do it with thy might, for there is no work nor device nor wisdom nor knowledge in the grave whither thou goest.' That last is something to be thankful for, anyhow," she added bitterly.

Gilles sat silent. She turned to him impulsively.

"That was foolishly spoken, Gilles. Abelard used to say one found the truth of one's self with you. There is a kind of satisfaction in doing one's work. And I try to train the novices, as Godric trained me. But the sisters—I have very little power over them. They go behind me to the Abbess. And you know how it is: there is a little spurt of authority, to give a permission that I have not given. She is like a child. The discipline of the house is like a rotten floor. And all the while Suger at St. Denis bides his time."

"I had meant to warn you against him, Heloise. You know already?"

"I know that he says he has found a deed proving that Argenteuil is a priory of St. Denis: and that he is only waiting till his case is complete before he turns us out. He is collecting every story that he hears. And I am afraid some of them are true."

"But what would become of you?"

She looked across the little strait to the black piles of turf and faggots on the deserted island. "Some of the sisters will go to other houses. Sometimes I think that perhaps the rest of us, the novices, and some of the old women, that knew Godric, might have a little house, away from Paris. A little thatched house. And dig our own garden and grow our own lettuce. And I could have hens. It would be no grief to me to leave Argenteuil."

"Heloise, do you remember in that room yonder Bernard of Clairvaux said that some day you would be an Abbess—that some day he would call you sister?"

Heloise nodded, her face expressionless.

" 'Let you once give,' " went on Gilles musingly, " 'you give for eternity.' "

[273]

She smiled again, the old defiant smile.

"And I said, 'But what if there is nothing left to give?' "

"Then . . . there is nothing, Heloise?"

"Nothing. How should there be? I took the veil, not for God's sake, but for Abelard's. What should I expect from God? I have done nothing for love of Him. If there is any merit in keeping vows once you have made them, in not being an open scandal to your profession, that perhaps I have. But it is a heathen virtue, that, not a Christian."

"That is not the reputation you have, Heloise. The common people, and they are the best judges, say you are a saint. They say that there is no beggar comes to the gate at Argenteuil but leaves it blessing you: that they bring you wailing children, and they are quiet in your arms: they are wounded, and your hands make whole."

She dropped her head in her hands and was silent for a while. "It is only the happy who are hard, Gilles. I think perhaps it is better for the world if—if one has a broken heart. One is quick to recognize it, elsewhere. And one has time to think about other people, if there is nothing left to hope for any more. Besides—if you saw them. Gilles, you do not know, I never knew, that such things could be. St. Paul once said that he could wish himself accursed for his own people. So I think could I— if I were not accursed already."

Gilles looked at the bowed head. So vast a reverence swept upon his heart, that for a little while he could not speak. At last he found his voice, but the words came haltingly, strange words from him.

"*Lord, when saw we thee an hungered and fed thee, or thirsty, and gave thee drink?*"

She started, her head like a stag's.

"No. No. You must not say that. It is not for me. But, Gilles, we are only wasting time. You know what I am here for. The children are only an excuse. Have you any news?"

Gilles nodded.

"Thibault was here yesterday. Child—I seem to be quoting Scripture freely today—do you remember '*Seek first the Kingdom of God, and all these things shall be added unto you*'?"

"Well?"

"You know he went to the woods at the Arduzon, to live in solitude. '*I said, I will go softly all my days in the bitterness of my soul.*' Well, do not ask me to explain it to you, for these things are beyond my understanding. But the thing that happened to St. Paul on the road to Damascus, and to St. Augustine, and to Isaiah in the year that King Uzziah died, has happened to him. He has seen God."

Heloise sat silent, her eyes burning on his face.

"He came back, content only to worship. But he changed the name of the oratory he had built of reeds and thatch for the Holy Trinity, to a new name, the oratory of the Paraclete, the Comforter. Two days after a couple of lads on their way from Troyes to the schools here lost their way in the woods, and came to the hut asking shelter for the night, thinking it was a charcoal burner's, and found him there. They came on the next day to Paris, with their news. And—you must have seen it for yourself, riding through this morning—the schools

[275]

are empty. They have flocked to him from Paris and
Orleans and Laon and Tours—aye, and Rheims. They
have built themselves huts of turf and reeds like his own.
They say it is a second Thebaid. He flung the world
away—and behold he draws all men after him."

Her eyes had widened, her lips parted. Gilles turned
away his eyes. It was a glory, but the glory of the woman
hearing praise of her lover.

"Gilles, have you a letter?"

He nodded. Then silently, he felt for it under the rug
and handed it to her. She began reading half aloud.

"*We are justified . . . in that by the life and death of
His Son He has so bound us to Himself that love so
kindled will shrink from nothing for His sake.*" Her voice
fell flat and dead.

Suddenly she thrust the letter from her into Gilles's
hand.

"Tell me, Gilles. It will be quicker. I cannot bear to
read it. Does he speak of me?"

He looked down at the letter, twisting it in his hands.
"Not yet," he said, very low.

She got up quickly and crossed the room to the window, that he might not see her agony. And standing
there, struggling to control herself, she heard behind
her a small stifled sound. She turned round. He had his
face to the wall, but she could see the old Silenus mask
distorted with soundless weeping, the hands opening and
closing in impotent despair. She was on her knees beside
him now, pressing his hands to her lips, her chin, her
cheek.

"Don't, Gilles. Beloved, you must not. You must not.
Dear Gilles, it was only for a moment. It is over now. It

does not hurt, now." Suddenly she stopped and gazed at him, something like bewilderment in her eyes. "Gilles, did you hear what I said? I only said it to comfort you. But it has come true. I can bear it now, because—because of you."

He was silent for a while, rubbing his eyes with his sleeve.

"Is that true, Heloise?"

"It is true. Though why it should be—why you must break your heart to comfort mine—"

He looked up, the old speculative gleam kindling in his eyes.

" 'Cuius dolore plaga nostra curata est; et lapsus nostros aliena ruina suscepit.' I read it, fifty years ago, in an old missal at Bobbio. They say St. Columban wrote it. They never use it now. 'By whose grief our wound was healed: by whose ruin our fall was stayed.' I wonder. Is that what men have always asked of God?"

PRODUCTION NOTES

DESIGNER: Maurice Serle Kaplan

TYPE: Linotype *Janson* with *Eve* decorative capitals.

TYPESETTING, ELECTROTYPING, PRINTING, AND BINDING: Quinn & Boden Co., Inc., Rahway, N. J.